GREAT EASTERN RAILWAY.

SEA-SIDE, & BROADS & RIVERS OF NORFOLK & SUFFOLK.

Tourist, Fortnightly, and Friday to Tuesday Tickets

ARE ISSUED AS UNDER BY ALL TRAINS:—

LIVERPOOL STREET OR ST. PANCRAS TO	Tourist.		Fortnightly.		Friday to Tuesday.	
	1 Class.	3 Class.	1 Class.	3 Class.	1 Class.	3 Class.
Hunstanton ... ... • ...	30 6	18 0	25 0	13 0	15 0	9 6
Lowestoft	33 0	19 9	27 6	15 0	20 0	10 0
Yarmouth	34 0	20 0	27/6	15/0	20/0	10/0
Cromer, Mundesley-on-Sea, or Wroxham	34/0	20 0	27/6	15/0	20/0	10/0
Norwich	31/10	18/11	—	—	—	—
LIVERPOOL STREET TO						
Southend-on-Sea ... ... / Burnham-on-Crouch	8/3	4 4	7/0	4/4	6/0 •	3/6
Walton-on-the-Naze, Clacton-on-Sea, Frinton-on-Sea, Harwich, or Dovercourt	20 0	12/0	17 6	10 0	12/6	7/6
Felixstowe	22/1	14 3	17 6	10/0	12 6	7 6
Aldeburgh	27 [illegible]	16 [illegible]	25 0	13 0	15 0	9 6
Southwold	31 3	18/[illegible]	27 6	15 0	20 0	10 0

TOURIST TICKETS are issued daily throughout the year by any train, and are available for the return journey by any train as follows:—Those issued from 1st May to the 31st of October inclusive, on any day up to and including the 31st of December of the year of issue. Those issued from 1st November to 30th April inclusive, on any day within two calendar months from the date of issue.

FORTNIGHTLY TICKETS are issued daily, and are available for return any day within 15 days, including days of issue and return.

FRIDAY TO TUESDAY TICKETS are issued every Friday and Saturday, and are available for return on the day of issue, or on any day up to and including the following Tuesday.

Tourist, Fortnightly, and Friday to Tuesday Tickets to the above Stations are also issued from Great Eastern Stations within 12 miles of London at the same fares as from Liverpool Street. Passengers are allowed to travel to and from Liverpool Street to join or leave the fast Sea-Side Trains; also to and from Stratford to join or leave the Trains booked to call at that Station. They are also issued from New Cross (L. B. & S. C.) and all Stations on the East London Railway, at the same fares as Liverpool Street.

The above Tickets are available to and from additional Stations as follows:— *Southend-on-Sea Tickets* at Prittlewell; *Burnham-on-Crouch Tickets* at Fambridge, Althorne, Southminster; *Clacton-on-Sea Tickets* at Frinton, Walton, Harwich, Dovercourt; *Walton-on-the-Naze Tickets* at Frinton, Clacton, Harwich, Dovercourt; *Frinton-on-Sea Tickets* at Clacton, Walton, Harwich, Dovercourt; *Harwich Tickets* at Dovercourt, Parkeston, Frinton, Clacton, Walton; *Felixstowe Tickets* at Trimley, Harwich; *Aldeburgh Tickets* at Leiston; *Southwold Tickets* at Darsham, Wenhaston, Blythburgh, Walberswick; *Hunstanton Tickets* at Heacham; *Lowestoft Tickets* at Beccles, Reedham, Carlton Colville, Oulton Broad, Yarmouth, Mundesley-on-Sea, Cromer; *Yarmouth Tickets* at Beccles, St. Olaves, Reedham, Acle, Lowestoft, Mundesley-on-Sea, Cromer; *Cromer Tickets* at Mundesley-on-Sea, Gunton, Yarmouth, Lowestoft; *Mundesley-on-Sea Tickets* at Yarmouth, Lowestoft, and Cromer. Passengers must pay the ordinary local single fares when travelling from one Station to the other.

Extra Journey Return Tickets at Reduced Fares are issued at the above Stations, except Southend-on-Sea and Burnham-on-Crouch, to the Station from which the Tickets were issued, to holders of not less than two Tourist or Fortnightly Tickets.

Extension of Tickets—Passengers holding Friday to Tuesday Tickets and wishing to stay for a Fortnight or a shorter period, may do so by paying the difference between the Friday to Tuesday and Fortnightly Fares; and in the same manner Fortnightly Tickets may be extended to Tourist Tickets by paying the difference between those fares.

Liverpool Street Station, 1[illegible]. **WILLIAM BIRT,** *General Manager.*

List of Farmhouse and Country Lodgings in the Eastern Counties, and Pamphlets on the "Broads" District of Norfolk and Suffolk can be obtained (post free) on application to the Superintendent of the Line, Liverpool Street Station, London, E.C.

PREFACE TO NEW EDITION

Poppy-Land is the name, given to Cromer and its vicinity, by the author and drama critic, Clement Scott. Following a short excursion to this 'pretty watering place', he was inspired to write a holiday article for The Daily Telegraph. This, published at the end of August, 1883, was to be the first of his Poppy-Land Papers, which appeared collectively three years later.

Scott's enthusiasm for the area was persuasive and the once secluded and peaceful corner of the Norfolk coast soon became a fashionable resort. The honest miller, Alfred Jermy, and his daughter, Louie, of whom Scott wrote, became celebrities; their home, Mill House, became a centre for visiting literati; china, festooned with poppies, Poppy-Land postcards and even Poppyland Bouquet perfume and soap, were eagerly sought souvenirs.

A favourite with the summer visitors was Scott's poem, The Garden of Sleep. It described the graveyard surrounding the lone cliff-top tower, at Sidestrand, which toppled over the edge in 1916. The 14th century church, St Michael's, to which that tower had been a comparatively new addition, was removed, brick by brick from its precarious perch, to a safer site barely three years before Scott's first visit there. Scott returned time and again to the forsaken 'garden', his special place, which, over the years, became the focal point of the Poppy-Land legend.

Clement Scott died on 25th June, 1904, but his influence has survived. The name Poppy-Land is still widely used; Cromer's museum features an exhibit on the author's life and times; books and pamphlets are available locally and, in 1985, the BBC televised a dramatised version of Scott's connection with the area. Understandably many visitors have looked for copies of the original Poppy-Land book which has been long out of print and extremely difficult to find. It is hoped, then, that this new edition will, as well as amending this, provide a particularly appropriate souvenir of Poppy-Land.

CHRISTINE STOCKWELL

I HAVE TO THANK MY UNTIRING FRIEND,

MR. J. M. LEVY,

AND

THE PROPRIETORS OF "THE DAILY TELEGRAPH"

FOR ONCE MORE

CHEERING THE MONOTONY OF WORK

WITH

A HAPPY INTERLUDE OF REST

AMONGST

FIELDS AND FLOWERS,

AND FOR

PERMITTING ME TO COLLECT THESE FUGITIVE THOUGHTS

INTO SO

UNWORTHY A GARLAND OF RECOLLECTION.

C. S.

"The Ruined ivy-covered Church at Overstrand"—*p.* 25.

POPPY-LAND

PAPERS DESCRIPTIVE OF SCENERY ON THE EAST COAST

BY

CLEMENT SCOTT

ILLUSTRATED BY F. H. TOWNSEND

"The Windmill seen for miles around"—p. 27.

First published 1886 by Carson & Comerford
Published 1894 and onwards by Jarrold & Sons
Re-published 1992 by Christine Stockwell

Reprinted 2000
Reprinted 2016

ISBN 978-0-9516640-2-5

CONTENTS.

POPPY-LAND.

A Prelude.

The Garden of Sleep!

A SUMMER SONG.

"Wherever men are noble they love bright colour: and where-ever they can live healthily, bright colour is given them in sky, sea, flowers, and living creatures!"

RUSKIN, "On Poppies." [Proserpina.]

ON the grass of the cliff, at the edge of the steep,
God planted a garden—a garden of sleep!
'Neath the blue of the sky, in the green of the corn,
It is there that the regal red poppies are born!
Brief days of desire, and long dreams of delight,
They are mine when my Poppy-Land cometh in sight.
In music of distance, with eyes that are wet,
It is there I remember, and there I forget!
O! heart of my heart! where the poppies are born,
I am waiting for thee, in the hush of the corn.
Sleep! Sleep!
From the Cliff to the Deep!
Sleep, my Poppy-Land,
Sleep!

In my garden of sleep, where red poppies are spread,
I wait for the living, alone with the dead!
For a tower in ruins stands guard o'er the deep,
At whose feet are green graves of dear women asleep!
Did they love as I love, when they lived by the sea?
Did they wait as I wait, for the days that may be?
Was it hope or fulfilling that entered each breast,
Ere death gave release, and the poppies gave rest?
O! life of my life! on the cliffs by the sea,
By the graves in the grass, I am waiting for thee!
Sleep! Sleep!
In the Dews by the Deep!
Sleep, my Poppy-Land,
Sleep!

The Garden of Sleep—*p.* 31.

The Cottage by the Mill!

IT was during my rambles round the East Coast of England some years ago that I chanced to find such an exceptionally-favoured and smiling corner, a village so secluded and at peace, surrounded by fields already ripe for the harvest within full view of the summer sea, that it struck me some description of life in an English farmhouse at harvest-time might have a passing interest to many on their rambles, and to many more over the fireside when returned to work again. The experience of a holiday spent amidst the most beautiful scenery of my own country, of walks from village to village, of many wanderings on down and cliff, of life at watering places, both fashionable and dull, at home and abroad, leads me to the conclusion that many a traveller in search of health and rest might do worse than change the restlessness and excitement of travel for the seclusion and stillness of an English farm in a village by the sea. As every summer comes round people are never tired of recommending to one another some quiet spot where they can live undisturbed by the great procession of tourists, a place where a table d' hôte is unknown, and the front door is free from the confusion of arriving and departing guests, a clean, quiet, homelike dwelling where literally you can take your ease at your inn. Never a year passes but some such discovery is made, only to be communicated to a few confidential friends. The theory is that when a pretty spot becomes known and popular it is spoiled. I must own that many such confidences have been duly communicated to me, but what has surprised me most is that the United Kingdom is supposed to be outside the regions of romance and retirement.

From time to time it has been whispered in my ear that if I really enjoy solitude and fine air, scenery, and seclusion, I shall find it at some "pension" on the Jura Mountains remote from the ordinary Swiss route, in the Maderanerthal Valley half-way up the St. Gothard pass, deep in the heart of the Black Forest at Wolfach, where they brew excellent German beer, at Triberg, where they make the cuckoo clocks, or at Rippoldsau, where they take delicious pine baths for chronic or occasional rheumatism. I have been recommended villages innumerable in many a Swiss canton, inns on the margin of as many Swiss lakes. I have been promised rest in the Island of Man and welcome banishment in the Island of Sark. I have no reason whatever to doubt the good faith of any of my informants, but it must never be forgotten that each and all of these enchanted peace-spots can only be arrived at after hours of agony by sea, or nights of dusty torture in a railway train; you have to get there with difficulty and to return with fatigue. How is it that we so often turn our tired eyes from these green islands of ours, forgetting that we, too, possess forests and mountains and deep dark valleys, that we have woods full of wild flowers almost untraversed by human foot, and hills of heather left to the birds and the bees? We steam up the Righi by a mountain railway to see the sun rise above the Alps, but never care to see the same sun ascending from the green sea that encircles our islands; we praise waterfalls abroad and leave our own mountain torrents unvisited; we almost persistently forget that within a couple of miles of some of the most fashionable and popular watering places in England there are villages, old churches, dreamy farms, flowered lanes, coppices, woods, and miles of heather land that are as empty and untenanted as if they were far removed from the confines of civilisation.

It was on one of the most beautiful days of the lovely month of August, a summer morning with a cloudless blue sky overhead and a sea without a ripple washing on the yellow sands, that I turned my back on perhaps the prettiest watering-place of the East Coast and walked along the cliffs to get a blow and a look at the harvest that had just begun. It was the old story. At a mile removed from the seaside town I had left I did not find a human being. Below me. as I rested among the fern on the lighthouse cliff, there they all were, digging on the sands, playing lawn tennis, working, reading, flirting, and donkey-riding, in a circle that seemed to me ridiculously small as I looked at it from this height. In that red-roofed village, the centre of all that was fashionable and select, there was not a bed to be had for love or money; all home comforts, all conveniences to which well-bred people were accustomed were deliberately sacrificed for the sake of a lodging amongst a little society that loved its band, its pier, its shingle, and its sea.

A mile away there were farmhouses empty, cottages to let, houses to be hired for a song; a mile to the right there were sands with no human being on them, deserted cliffs, empty caves, unfrequented rocks; a mile to the left there was not a footprint on the beach, not a foot-fall on the grassy cliff. Custom had established a certain fashion at this pretty little watering-place, and it was religiously obeyed; it was the rule to go on the sands in the morning, to walk on one cliff for a mile in the afternoon, to take another mile in the opposite direction at sunset, and to crowd upon the little pier at night. But the limit was a mile either way. No one thought of going beyond the lighthouse; that was the boundary of all investigation. Outside that mark the country, the farms, and the villages were as lonely as in the Highlands.

In aimless fashion I strolled on, and attracted by a ruined church tower, took a cut through the cornfields towards a cluster of farms and a distant village. It is difficult to convey an idea of the silence of the fields through which I passed, or the beauty of the prospect that surrounded me—a blue sky without a cloud across it; a sea sparkling under a haze of heat; wild flowers in profusion around me, poppies predominating everywhere, the hedgerows full of blackberry-blossom and fringed with meadow-sweet; the bees busy at their work, the air filled with insect life, the song-birds startled from the standing corn as I pursued my solitary way. So great was the change from the bustle of fashion to this unbroken quiet that I could scarcely believe that I was only parted by a dip of coast line from music and laughter and seaside merriment, from bands and bathing machines, from crochet and circulating libraries. Walking to the cliff's edge, I found a deserted sand; looking across the fields there was no sound but the regular click of the reaping machine under which the golden grain was falling.

It was just the time of day when an English farm has such a sleepy look. No one seemed about anywhere as I surveyed the farm buildings, no voice broke the silence. The men and labourers were far afield busy with the reaping, and the barns were wide open for the first loads of the harvest. An old horse came to look at me and put his nose over the gate of an adjacent field; the fowls were busy in the stubble where the barley had just been cut; and on the grass plot in front of the silent farmhouse a deserted tennis net was the

"An old horse came to look at me"—*p.* 8.

only sign of civilisation. The contemplation of this homestead, close by a ruined church mantled in ivy, the solitude of its surroundings, the silence of the scene suggested the charm of such a life. But it was no use applying for lodgings or farmhouse accommodation at such a spot as this; if I was destined to be housed anywhere it must be in a place of quite another pattern. So I pursued my journey in a contented frame of mind in the direction of the nearest village. Even the village itself contained few signs of the stir of human life. A small circle of children, released from school, were resting from the sun under the shade of the roadside hedge; a cart waited at the door of the village inn. But not a face was to be seen at any cottage window; the fishermen were away trawling in the North Sea, and there was uncommonly little trade at the village shop set back in a garden full of homely cottage flowers. At last my patience was rewarded. Half a mile beyond the deserted village, at a bend of the road under the shadow of a windmill, there was presented to my sight what appeared to be a very cosy spot.

It was one of those farmhouses that is

the exact reproduction of the style of cottage that all children are set to draw when they commence their first lesson. A little red-brick house with three white windows on the first floor, a little white door in the middle, a window at either side, and a stack of chimneys at each end of the cottage. The house was divided from the road by a white gate and palings, and in the enclosure was a garden brilliant with flowers. I could not resist the temptation of leaning over the white gate in order to contemplate so peaceful a scene. On the right of the gate was a bright bed of yellow evening primrose scattered among the low fruit bushes; on the left was a kitchen garden divided from the circular grass plot by rose trees, and in the middle was a perfect holiday ground for bees, a brilliant bed made up of geranium, calceolaria, phlox, clarksia, and French marigold. This was evidently the miller's house, for it was not fifty yards from the slope of cornfield that was topped by the windmill, and here I thought I might venture to suggest the desired accommodation which had been everywhere denied me at the adjacent seaside town. My question was met with that natural courtesy and cheerfulness that seem to be characteristic of the county of Norfolk. I may pause here to remark upon a most pleasant feature of country life in this hospitable district. You never pass along the road morning, noon, or night without being treated to a cheery greeting; it is either a good morning or a good night, a chat about the weather or the crops, a bow from the lads or a curtsey from the lasses, as the stranger threads his way among the Norfolk lanes. I never felt more at home in my life or was made more welcome than in my wanderings in East Anglia. These things seem small and immaterial, but life goes along somehow more pleasantly when the labourer trudging to his toil in the morning can exchange greetings with his neighbour, and when at nightfall a gruff "Goodnight" comes out of the darkness of the road as people pass on their way homewards.

"Could I be allowed a lodging for a few days?"

"Indeed you could," was the answer of the miller's daughter, who opened the hospitable white door of the farmhouse that sunny morning. The family that had occupied the house all the summer had just gone away, and father would be delighted to have me as a temporary tenant. I was told that father would not quarrel about terms; that the fare at the farm was simple enough, but that everyone would do their best for me; that I could come in at once, that very night if I liked, for all the rooms were ready, and that father was the fortunate possessor of a fast grey pony and a basket chaise, quite strong enough to bring me over with my traps whenever I cared to order it. Need I say that I closed with the offer at once. A farmhouse within two fields of the sea, a garden full of flowers and fruit, a bed-room spotlessly clean, with a full view of the windmill and the cornfields, a sitting-room full of old oak and old-fashioned furniture, country lanes bright with poppies and the wild Michael-mas daisy, not a sound but the drone of bees in the flower beds and the busy presence of insect life, a hospitable host glad to welcome me and a civil little daughter determined to make me comfortable, early to bed and early to rise—these were some of the advantages held out in prospect to me. Times out of number I have crossed the Channel and travelled many a weary mile in search of some such place as was here ready to hand in my native land. How far my ideas were fulfilled, and how pleasant holiday life can become in such a retreat, I shall presently describe in greater detail.

Four-in-hand in Poppy-Land.

A Day in Poppy-Land

THE honest miller who lived in the farm by the sea was as good as his word. The wind was slack, and the corn around his little homestead scarcely ripe, so he duly presented himself with the basket-carriage and the fast-trotting pony to fetch me away from the monotonous existence of a seaside resort to the more simple pleasures of a sunny country life. We can do original things in these primitive parts, and so it did not seem at all odd to the inhabitants of the seaside village pretending to be fashionable to see a dusty miller convoying his guest to his distant home. It was just the evening for a drive in the country; the sun had set, the bright, clear flame of the lighthouse flashed now to sea and now across the peaceful country, the yellow evening primrose was opening in the cottage gardens, and the last wagons laden with sheaves were coming home to the barns from the fields. I left my seaside friends as I had found them, doing as little as they could with monotonous regularity. There was a moon in the heavens, acres and acres of woodland within an easy walk of the hotels and lodging-houses, cliffs to climb although the day was done, and yet no one ventured to depart from the monotony of the orthodox seaside programme. They had done their sands, done their cliff, called for their letters at the village post-office, read their newspapers, eaten their accustomed meals, and now there was nothing to be accomplished except to walk on a wooden pier and to listen to the music of an active but not very distinguished band. "If you are not in a hurry for time, I can take you a pretty drive to the mill," observed my host, as he allowed the old pony clearly to see that he was on his way homewards; and the worthy miller was right. We took a road that led through a wood, not quite deserted yet by the light, and passed one of the show cottages of the district, a gabled pleasaunce with a rustic porch, built in a hollowed clearance of some noble trees, sheltered by rhododendrons and azaleas, and now showing an added charm owing to the lights in the latticed windows. If the old mill farm looked homely enough in the

An evening drive with an honest miller—*p.* 13.

full glare of the midday sun, with a bright light upon the flower beds, and the business of the day, such as it was, in full swing, you can imagine the hospitable look of it as we drove up to the white rustic gate and saw through an open window a supper table spread with a fair white linen cloth, candles lighted, and vases of wild flowers for simple decoration. It was just the room in which such a homely table should have been arranged. The furniture was of old solid oak of antique pattern; a combined chest of drawers and escritoire contained the odd books that seemed to have been left by successive reading parties, but in reality had been purchased by the miller at farm-house sales which he loved to frequent; religion and classics hopelessly mixed, Ovid side by side with Baxter's sermons, and theological dissertations in friendly companionship with Todhunter's Algebra. For pictures there were the coloured illustrations from many a Christmas number of the "Illustrated London News" and the "Graphic," framed by the miller during his winter evenings, some German reproductions of Raffaelle's cartoons, and a wonderful series of coloured plates representing the virtues of a temperate man contrasted with the wretched career of a drunkard, on the true Hogarthian model. The little drawing-room on the other side of the entrance-door was an apartment evidently held in greater respect and even reverence. It smelt of lavender, and was spotlessly clean; the horsehair sofa was an imposing piece of furniture, the carpet had evidently been a study in green and gold, flowers had been placed in every corner of the room, photographs of the miller's family and ancestors hung upon the walls, together with many religious prints, coloured and plain; and on a special table in the corner of the room lay in state the huge family Bible. The miller's house, though compact and regular in front, was roomy at the rear, and capable of holding a decent-sized family of children and nurses, if their parents were only sensible enough to bring them here instead of into stuffy, unwholesome lodgings. As for my bedroom, it was almost wholly occupied by a comfortable old-fashioned tent bedstead, but it looked to the front—a south-west aspect—and the road was lost in the interval between the miller's garden and the acres of ripe corn on the slope of the mill-hill.

"Could I eat eggs and bacon," was the modest request, as the miller's daughter uncovered a smoking dish, and pointed to the farmhouse bread and fresh butter. What could I not have eaten here, so admirably contrasted as it all was in its homeliness and comfort with the very undesirable food, the secondhand table d'hôte, the inevitable discomfort of crowded hotels and hurried waiters, which I had exchanged for this elysium. And, maybe, I could enjoy also, after this frugal and wholesome supper, leaning over the white garden gate and looking up to the sails of the silent mill, that last evening pipe that always seems sweeter in the country air, and prepares the holiday-maker for a good seven hours of unbroken rest. So grateful was the rest, indeed, that it was soon evident that further sleep was impossible after seven o'clock in the morning. The prospect of a good breeze had stirred the miller early to set the sails going and begin on the new corn, which had already come up from the fields. The first farm wagons were soon passing the miller's gate, and the swallows were chasing one another under the eaves of the country cottage. But the chance of a dip in the sea was the first consideration. Two fields led me to the edge of the cliff, and a circuitous path down the sandy face of it took me safely down to the utterly deserted beach.

Here there was a chance of a swim such as bathers seldom find. Three miles along the coast it would have been necessary to wait in turn for a bathing machine, to bribe the proprietor for preference, and to be strictly confined to the very proper regulations made at such places. But what a change here! Had I been cast on a desert island I could not have been more alone. Not a human being on the cliff, not a house or cottage to be seen, not a footfall on the beach, a cave to use as a dressing-room, and mile after mile of virgin sand, unsoiled by stone or pebble, to run upon in the sun and in the breeze after coming out of the water. At ordinary seaside places a sea-bath cannot possibly be followed by an air bath, which is just as valuable to the health and constitution; but here, in this deserted nook, I can honestly say that I have never seen a human creature since I changed my quarters. A bath of this pattern naturally leads to a breakfast with an appetite to which most Londoners are strangers, and after breakfast, at the request of the miller, I go up to the old mill to be weighed, to see a splendid view of sea and cornfield from one of the upper storeys, and to be initiated in the art of making flour under the process that has existed for some hundreds of years, and is now only gradually dying out. For the first time for many weeks the old mill was going, the new corn was pouring in, and my host was anticipating a brisk sale for his flour, his bran, and his pollard, which he sold retail to his country neighbours. Here the good fellow had worked contentedly for many a year, attending to the entire mill himself, and often in the winter-time working morning and night in these whitened chambers and preparing for that rainy day, to him a windless week, when trade must necessarily stop. Standing that sunny morning with the blue sea before me and the smiling landscape round about, with the whirling sails rushing through the air, I wondered if these old-fashioned windmills, dotted all over England, could ever be utilised for the collection and storage of one of the forces that are in time to supersede steam. It would be decidedly an original idea to collect force at a country windmill, to pack it up on the spot, and to deliver it, carriage paid, by the parcels post.

The next visit was, of course, to the harvest field, where on all sides they were gathering in the grain with extraordinary rapidity, owing to the general use of machinery for cutting and storing. During my visit to these districts I did not see a single farm on which labour was employed for mowing and reaping, and now-a-days every farmer with a fair acreage uses his own machinery, and does not share it with his neighbours, according to the old plan. I passed an old man, a man of some seventy odd summers, sitting on a stile as he surveyed the harvest operations, and he was fairly astonished at the rapidity with which the land was cleared as contrasted with his own recollections, but none the less inclined to favour what seemed to him the "new-fangled method." I have spoken elsewhere of the courtesy, and I might add the reverence of the Norfolk labourer, who seldom announces his determination of visiting any place on the morrow or going anywhere without the addition of "If God spares me, sir." And I might here note one of the curious harvest customs that must have come down direct from Norman times. When the reapers are in the field they are allowed, or rather it is the custom, to demand "largesse" from the passer-by. Indeed, the very same old French word is used. The phrase goes, "Please da me a largesse, sir!" which I made a brown-cheeked labourer translate—"Please give me something to drink

"Some seventy odd summers"—*p.* 20.

your jolly good health with." Not only the labourers in the field, but the children in the lanes ask for "largesse" at harvest time. The girls and boys, with eyes as black as sloes, follow the visitor with no cringing importunity, but a laughing downright request, such as "Please da me a copper, sir." The perpetuation to this very day of the latin "da," or "give me," is as curious as the retention of the French "largesse." It would be possible to walk for miles around this healthy and hospitable country without the slightest fatigue, amongst the crops and the cornfields, for here, as in Switzerland, the vigorous and bracing air deprives one of all sense of weariness. All the harvesting I have seen is done in full view of the sea; the crops grow to the very edge of the cliffs, which constantly exercise the inhabitants by crumbling away, making huge gaps and ravines of sandy soil, that are soon grown over by the poppy, the thistle, and the sea daisy. And then the landscape is so delightfully varied. Now you come across an old church tower, ivy grown and picturesque, surrounded by forgotten gravestones, and the matrices of old brasses, the last relic of the parish church, removed, like the lighthouse, further back upon the cliff, for fear its foundations shall totter and fall. Now you enter a village, and, desperately thirsty after those breakfast shrimps or Yarmouth bloater, beg for a drink of water, not lighting on any inn in this most temperate county, but finding a curious old cottage, with an old lady presiding over it who has passed the last fifty-seven years of her life under the same roof, never stirring far from the village, and living now in simple content on half a crown given her by the parish, supplemented by a share of the earnings of her grandson, a farm labourer, who has sworn never to marry whilst his old grandmother is alive. Of the temperance of these Norfolk labourers I can speak with experience. They do not apparently need blue ribbons or pledges to keep them sober. For the most part they drink water, because they like it and thrive upon it, and their potations even in the harvest field are very moderate. I have not seen a drunken man since I have been in the place, and have never yet passed a labourer at any time of the day without being saluted by him in a friendly fashion, and as if I, a stranger, was made welcome by the inhabitants. And so slip along with pleasant ease the wheels of a country day at harvest time. There is always something to see, ever something to be done. If tired of the farms and the cliffs, you can stroll down to the deserted beach, and obtain the freedom and space necessarily denied elsewhere. If the day is too hot for exercise the nights are at least supremely beautiful, whether viewed from the old mill mound, watching the fields illumined by the lighthouse tower, or from the cliff's edge when what they call here the "fisherman's moon" makes a pathway of gold across the waveless sea. Such is but a brief outline of existence at a place where there are fields to wander in, all untenanted, woods full of wild flowers that bloom unseen by human eye, cliffs that have no visitors but the sand marten and the swallow—a sea that is my only companion, and a sand that no one else cares to use as a playground. There are no children here, though there are farms in plenty to take them in, milk and eggs and butter to feed them with, gardens full of vegetables and flowers to delight them—no, the children are all packed away in lodgings that are unwholesome, and are swarming upon sands that are crowded; there are no "sympathies" here, though there are cliffs on which they could rest all day without an interloper near them—here, indeed, why the "sympathies" are proclaiming their affection publicly on the pier or esplanade, and dressing smart for one another's mutual satisfaction; there are no hard-worked fathers or harassed mothers here—no, they are wheeling perambulators on popular spas, and exposing to an astonished world the pranks of their unruly children. Youth and age, married and unmarried, take their holidays elsewhere, and have not yet discovered this Poppy-land, which, to state it practically, can be reached in five hours from Liverpool Street Station. Any one putting himself into a train at 3.30 might be opening the gate of the Old Mill Farm by eight o'clock, and by midnight reposing in Lavender and lost in dreamland.

Northrepps Cottage—*p.* 14.

Among the Corn Fields.

THERE are worse moments in the life of a man "who works and feels he works" than the awakening after ten good hours of refreshing and unbroken sleep, and the first bright peep of a summer landscape from the open window of a farm house by the sea. In this silent corner of East Anglia I appear to be at the very end of the world. It is as lonely as Tintagel, as breezy as Boscastle. Two miles away, over the ferncovered down, away by the ruined ivy-covered church at Overstrand and past the bright white light-house, that stands amidst acres of soft velvety turf and yellow sea daisies, the shrimp man and the lobster-catcher are arousing Cromer from its slumbers. The old church clock in the fine old flint tower, common to the county of Norfolk, is doubtless chiming eight, accompanied as an after thought by a few bars from Spohr's "As pants the hart;" they are taking down the shutters at the popular chemist's where everything is to be obtained, from patent pills to boot-blacking, and from calomel to curry powder. At Cromer they are getting out the early bathing machines; the coastguardmen on the cliff are surveying miles and miles of purple and waveless sea with an everlasting telescope; the crowded lodging houses and hotels are relieving themselves of the restless and the early risers; the market women are bringing in their little store of French beans, plums, and greengages. At Cromer already there is a stirring spirit and a suspicion of noise, a clattering of little spades and pails, and a scampering of sea babies to the yellow sands and the beneficent beach. In the farmhouse garden where I rest there is not a stir and not a sound. The front flower garden, separated from the road and its blackberry hedges by a row of white palings and a brighter white gate, seems revelling in the first touches of the August sunshine. Bees are busy with the lavender, and are coquetting with the brilliant French marigolds and deep purple carnations. The roses are almost over now, save on one low corner bush that will yield a yellow crop of Maréchal Niel from this moment until Christmas Day. A bed of mauve-coloured clarksia—the pride of our village—a rival bed decorated with stocks, verbenas, seedums, and the early-flowering asters are visited by bees and butterflies alike; the birds are calling one another from hedge to hedge, and so peaceful and beautiful is the scene that the darting house martens who have built in the eaves of the old farmhouse, although collecting for their departure to sunnier climes, seem disinclined to leave this warm corner of the England that they love. But look beyond the garden enclosure to the fields that slope towards the distant hills. On a small green platform crowning a field of waving barley stands the windmill seen for miles around, the most picturesque feature in this sunny landscape, and to our delight is seen whirling round in its old-fashioned way, careless of the counter advantages of machinery and steam. The good old miller has had no cause to regret the opening weeks of a fickle August. It has blown steadily, fitfully, and in gusts. Sometimes dark rain clouds have drifted from sea to hill, scattering spray or rain dust rather than rain. Sometimes a deep indigo thunder cloud has sailed from the west, emptying itself on the parched fields, rejoicing the hearts of the turnips and mangolds, but making little impression ten minutes afterwards on the dry and hungry soil. But whenever there has been sun—and we have not had too much of it this summer—there has been a bright, brisk breeze, bending down the apple trees in the garden, bowing down the corn in the fields, and sending the light fleecy clouds scudding along over the windmill top and away into the heart of the country. The young farmer next door is already out with his gun, stealing quietly by the hedge side up to the ferny plantation to see if he can catch a rabbit on the feed and help to stock the larder at home. Next month's Michaelmas geese are gobbling in the only field not under cultivation, keeping a respectful distance from a family of young turkeys growing up for next Christmas dinner, and paying no attention to the silent cattle or to the old mare with its young foal, who claim the privilege of eating their breakfast between the same hedges. So much for the front of the house this quiet summer morning. Let us look out at the back. See, we are only a couple of hundred yards from the cliff's edge, fringed with cornfields and decorated with scarlet poppies and mauve-coloured scabious. It will want another good ten days' sun to ripen the wheat, that now shows a lovely tone between dead green and a deep brownish yellow. From the upper windows I can see a vast expanse of purple ocean covered with herring boats starting on their annual journey to the North Sea, well manned with sailors from the little village yonder, whose wives will not see them again until Christmas time most likely, but every Saturday will punctually trudge to the agents at Cromer to draw their weekly house-money. Soon after Lammas Day they are all off, and cannot wait to give a hand at the oncoming harvest, even if they were wanted, for, to tell the truth, the farmer who is a practical man never calls upon the services of a sailor in the harvest field, unless he is uncommonly hard pressed. For Jack at home is a lazy, indolent fellow. I pass him every evening lolling under the thick-set hedge, I notice him in the morning stretched out among the poppies at the cliff's edge, watching the horizon, eternally looking out to sea, smoking innumerable pipes, and doing simply nothing in a magnificent manner. He is civil enough is the Norfolk sailor. He has always some pleasant salutation on his lips, he never fails to bid you good morning or good night though you pass him a dozen times a day, but when Jack is ashore he doesn't mean to work. The father of some sixty summers may bend his back in the fields from sunrise to sunset; the old mother may go out cleaning to the nearest farmer's, the wife may go down cliff and bring up pails of sea water for the young lady visitors at the arm; but the muscular young sailor only intends to be ornamental, not useful, when he is at home. His occupation is to stroll up to the look-out by the ruined tower and to watch the sea. How often when he is toiling on the deep must he have watched the land, and on a fine night seen the lights in the cottage windows where the lonely women are praying for the men at sea. It would be pleasant enough to waste hour after hour in the farmhouse garden to enjoy that first morning pipe under the old mill with some favourite book—we never get newspapers here until they are a day or so old—to trudge among the cornfields with the favourite little terrier at one's heels, who is death to field mice and a terror to moles; but there is the sea that can be reached by crossing only one cornfield, and there is no bathing round the coast of England to be compared to the stretch of deserted virgin sand untraversed by any human foot between the busy watering places of Cromer and Mundesley. But the sea below and the springs above, the beating of the waves, and the land water that pours down in torrents when it rains, are creating havoc with the Norfolk cliffs. Composed mainly of soft blue clay they yield at the pressure of every storm and are lessened by every tempest. Year follows year and acre after acre slips into the sea. The pathway we trod last year lies sheer down below a ruin of grass and wild flowers. The steps cut down the cliff for the children yesterday is to-day an impenetrable morass of crumbling clay. So serious has been the cliff fall eastward and westward from Cromer that the frightened villagers of our little hamlet have moved their tiny church a quarter of a mile landward, and have left their old tower and their buried dead enclosed in a churchyard doomed for destruction, but making in its loneliness and melancholy one of the most pathetic and picturesque corners of this land. For here there is always poetry and always peace. The seabirds whirl about the old church tower, the reapers reap, the sun alls, and nature is as silent as the grave. From here at night, when the sun has set over Cromer, the bright gleam of the white lighthouse, with its brilliant lamps, contrasts with the primrose tint of the distant sky, and makes nature a poem. Here, sitting on the old church wall later on, we see the bats flitter from the isolated tower, and the white owls swooping over the sailors' graves, and hear the last song of the reapers as they carry the last load home.

"Where are the bathing machines?" some one will ask, as he descends with difficulty the narrow path that the fishermen have cut in the crumbling cliff. Where, indeed! And what need of them? Between Cromer and Mundesley there may be an odd dozen or so tents, pitched here and there to accommodate the residents at the farm houses, but this, to all intents and purposes, is a deserted shore. The caves in the cliffs provide ample dressing rooms, and in the early morning, or at mid day for the matter of that, there is not a soul visible on cliff or sand. The island of Sark is not more desolate. So the bather, unrestricted by rules and regulations, can take his dip when and where he pleases, and enjoy the luxury of an air bath as well as a sea plunge. "A nice day for your washing," observed an old farm labourer whom I found tilling the soil at the cliff's edge one morning when I mounted from the beach. Out of breath with the climb I was glad of a rest, and he not altogether

"The late lingerer over the white farm-house gate"—*p.* 39.

indifferent for a chat and the price of a pint of ale when work was done. So we fell to chatting about the harvest prospects. He was veritably the oldest inhabitant. He had lived in our seaside village for sixty odd years, and was now toiling hard to support a wife, a married daughter, and an unfortunate son-in-law, and who shall say how many grandchildren who raced along the pathway in the yellow corn to greet the old man when he came from the parish church every Sunday afternoon. Dear me, what did he not remember? He remembered when the farmhouse was a splendid old hall—it had once been a monastery with images of saints in the niches of the walls; he remembered the destruction of two windmills at least by fire, and "a fine fire they made to be sure;" he remembered when there were eight or ten acres more cultivated land at the cliff's edge than there are now; and when such a thing as a railway from Norwich was never dreamed of. The old man was indifferently interested in politics, and did not appear to care a brass farthing whether he had a vote or not. He thought Liberals were as good as Conservatives, and vice-versa, but had somehow or other got it into his old head that the Conservatives were in favour of "a dear loaf!" He had no complaint to make about the "Parliament gentlemen," but necessarily got his political knowledge second-hand, as the old fellow could not read or write. Still, he wondered what the people who lived in towns would do for their bread if he didn't work all day in the fields, and seemed to imagine, as most toilers do, that he was the most wearily worked man in creation. My old friend was, albeit, a cheerful and garrulous old fellow. He envied his little grandchildren the gift of being able to read and write, for he lived in days when education was little thought of; but so long as by trimming the hedges, working in the field, taking a job whenever he could get it, and walking miles and miles to get work when it was slack, he could make up twelve or thirteen shillings a week to comfort the large family dependent on him he was not inclined to grumble. When I told him that he was to be envied for living in a healthy cottage by the sea, with its little flower garden about it; that he ought to be thankful for fresh air and the health-giving breezes of the coast, instead of being cramped up in a miserable garret in over-crowded London, he simply shook his head. What should he know of towns or the misery of great cities. In sixty years he had only once seen Norwich, an hour's journey by rail. As for London, I might as well have spoken of Melbourne for aught he knew or cared about it. But far beyond politics, the imminent elections, or the over-crowding of great cities, he was chiefly concerned with the vital question of harvest wages. The harvest wage, which is paid in a lump sum, is looked forward to by the Norfolk labourer as a means for paying the yearly rent of the cottage—say three pounds a year—and putting by something for a rainy day. Last year the farmers had paid seven pounds harvest money in this district, but just now a terrible rumour had been spread about from cottage to cottage that six pounds per man was to be the maximum wage given. The harvest labourers are hired with the earnest token of a shilling, as in the case of recruiting, and, as a rule, the farmers in the neighbourhood consult together and settle what amount of wages they can fairly afford. My old friend was terrified lest some misguided labourer should have in an unguarded moment taken the fatal six pounds and so compelled the rest to follow suit. "He may have been talked over with promises of beef in a barn and beer from the barrel when harvest is over," pleaded the ruddy-faced sexagenarian. They are very well in themselves, but won't pay the rent or keep the children, as he very wisely observed. However, I was pleased to hear afterwards that the rumour was ill-founded, and that when the harvest comes seven pounds a man will be paid down cheerfully by the farmers, as in the good old times, so there will be no grumbling or discontent.

The sun still shines by fits and starts, the breezes are boisterous, but though oats are cut down in some of the fields, the barley and wheat will want a good deal of scorching yet before they are ready for the sickle and the reaping machine. The harvest, which lasts a good month in most of the farms, is anxiously expected everywhere. No one can settle down until harvest is over. Directly the word is given for the men to go into the field a wave of excitement passes over the country. The children, much to their delight, are dismissed from school for a good five or six weeks, and the grave schoolmaster, at the head of the lads, chases the rabbits as they are turned out of the falling wheat and barley. Laughter and song are heard all over the land, louder than the wind that bends the ripening crops or the sea that moans at the foot of the crumbling cliffs. Then is the time for "largesse." It is the etiquette of harvest time in the Norfolk lands to demand "largesse" from every passing stranger. "Please da us largesse," say the urchins, boys, and girls, whilst the foreman of the gang of labourers will leave the sickle or the horse and ask the stranger alms for the toilers on the field. Later on, when the harvest is over, the oldest labourer of the village calls round at the various farms and houses and demands a more substantial form of "largesse," that is expended on a harvest supper at the village inn. It was on one of these visits that the oldest inhabitant insisted on singing to me an old Norfolk Harvest Song which he had learned fifty or sixty years ago. It is a quaint old ditty and is worth preserving now that village songs are forgotten and the labourer only cares for the latest music-hall doggerel or "Wait till the clouds roll by." Here is the old song:—

A NORFOLK HARVEST SONG.

Now Lammas Day is over, boys, we will begin,
We will cut down the corn, and carry it in;
We will reap, we will mow, we will sweat to the brow,
We will cut down the corn that so sweetly does grow.

We have an old man that is tilling the land—
His back it is bent, and he can scarcely stand-
He will get up in the morning and do all he can,
And pray God to reward the Old Harvest Man.

A man that is lazy and will not come in—
He will hinder his master, and likewise the men—
We will pay him his wages and bid him begone,
For what shall we do, lads, with such lazy one?

Now Harvest is ended, we will make a great noise,
And our master will say, "You are welcome, brave boys;"
We will broach the old Ale Tub, and box it along,
And now we will end the Old Harvest Song!

There is a good time coming no doubt, but men and lads alike will have to wait a little longer. Meanwhile the country round about is in its full glory of summer loveliness. The crops are changing from deep green to golden yellow, and the scarlet poppies are not yet faded or dead among the corn. The root crops, lately so parched, are refreshed by the recent rains, and the ferns on the hills, where the rabbits hide, stand out rich and green against a skyline of Eton blue. No moon has yet shone out at night over the churchyard by the sea, or made the farmhouse garden decorated with the pale evening primrose and its stars of midnight bloom as bright as day. But after sunset comes that strange white light of summer time, and the evening breezes bring a scent of ripening corn to the late lingerer over the white farm-house gate.

"Away go the labourers, with the old foreman at their head"—*p.* 47.

A Harvest Sun.

IT is half-past five o'clock on a lovely summer morning in mid-August. A crowd of labourers, headed by the foreman, is assembled under the farmer's window. Before the pluckiest or least sleepy of the band of early risers summons up courage to tap at the window-pane with the end of his scythe or to throw up a handful of pebbles or sand to awaken "the master," let me present to you in its full glory this lovely scene of incomparable English landscape. The farm labourer, if he only knew it, sees nature in her richest and purest attire. What money we spend; what dreary, dusty railway journeys we undergo; what a fuss and a fume we must get in; what conquering of languages and study of Bradshaw's Railway Guide, before we can see the sun rise on the Righi Mountain, or the sun sink, making the white snow roseate, over the Jungfrau at Interlaken. We clothe ourselves with borrowed blankets at

"5.30 a.m."—*p.* 40.

the Righi-Kulm. An electric bell rings, and there is a hustling of humanity, a clattering of cosmopolitan boots. It is like leaving a bathing machine for a plunge in the sea. We hesitate as to the expediency of leaving purses and valuables in the deserted hotel bed-room. And all for what? To see the sun rise sulkily or beautifully over the series of snow peaks, or to get back to bed disappointed laden with spoils from the bric-à-brac stalls that have been driving a roaring trade under the patronage of the semi-somnolent Britisher. I can give you as good a sunrise for a few shillings. I can promise you more beauty and less inconvenience in the matter of sunrises and sunsets at our Norfolk village, that can be reached in four or five hours from the Liverpool-street or St. Pancras stations. The sun rises here as at the Righi. Here over the sea; there over the mountains. Here over countless acres of wheat and barley; there over snow peaks and a glorious panorama of distance. All idea of foul weather has disappeared. The rain clouds have sailed away. The sea has become calm as a mill-pond. The wind has tried every quarter, but at last it has settled down to a dead calm. The sails of the old mill overlooking the silent farm refuse to stir. There is sunlight on sea and on cliff; sunlight dancing down the deserted lanes; sunlight travelling fast over the fern-covered hills; sunlight beating against the windows of the sleep-haunted farm. If that old foreman of the farm could only appreciate Nature, that is ever with him, as we can love it who have it not, what wonderful stories he would have to tell of the summer mornings he has trudged from his cottage in the village to wake the master at the farm. Already the birds are in full song in the hedges, and the bees are busy in the strawberry-tinted blossoms of the blackberries. The farmer's cocks and hens have taken a fancy to roosting in the young oak and blackthorn opposite the farm gate, and are now wending their way in procession to the farmyard to see what is going on and to pay a morning call to the geese, the turkeys, and the ducks who are paddling in the slush or mirroring their white or parti-coloured breasts in the farmyard pond on which the morning sun is shining. Already a farm labourer who has got his orders overnight is tethering the oxen and horses in a grass field; the farm boys and the labourers' children, turned out of bed at cock crow, are off to the cliff's edge to look out to sea, or to slide down the sand slopes for want of something better to do. All the village is awake, save the visitors at the farm, who are sleeping peacefully behind those white blinds on which the morning sun flings its reproachful rays. Why should they not sleep? The hard-worked clergyman is here, worn out with his London ministering, enjoying his summer holiday, though the perambulating postman tells me he delivers to him "over a score letters" every morning; the young wife is here—she cannot be more than three-and-twenty—and I saw her this morning wending her way to the sea with two little children who could scarcely toddle, a baby in arms, and a patient husband, who carried an early luncheon in a lawyer's brief bag; tired, rest-hunting brain workers are here, scattered about the two or three sea-side farms that compose our village. Why should they not sleep, poor things, seeing that it is as yet but half-past four o'clock in the morning?

The labourer's day is different from ours. He has seen the country all his life, and is apparently sick of it. He would rather have one hour in London than a whole summer day in the Norfolk village. He cannot understand or even dimly appreciate this delightful rest. They missed me for a few days from my accustomed haunts, and when I was back again they one and all "hoped I had enjoyed myself when I was up in London." It was to them an ambition—to me a necessity. But the labourers, for all they may tell you to the contrary, thrive well on the fresh air and the sea breezes. Their children have no ache or ailment. The youngest mother is up and about within a few days of her latest trouble. Their wages scarcely ever run to a pound a week; but the food they eat is wholesome, the air they breathe is sweet; they have kind friends at the parsonage or the big house to look after them when they are in trouble; they can raise flowers and grow vegetables; their cottages are bright in front with marigold and lavender, and well stocked behind with French beans and potatoes and vegetable marrow. Each tiny homestead is furnished with its cottage garden, and when I see these healthy labourers, their buxom wives, and strong-limbed children, I cannot find it in my utmost sympathy to pity these tillers of the soil, notwithstanding the fact of their twelve odd shillings a week wage and abated harvest money. I have seen in my time other working men leaving their homes at half-past five o'clock in the morning; but that was in London, and not in a seaside village. I have seen issuing from courts and alleys, from filthy squares and frowsy tenements, the men who go forth to their work and their labour at the only hour when London can ever be pure and beautiful. The sunrise, in its transcendent beauty, appears to purify the wretchedness of yesterday. All the sins and oaths and uncleanness of the last night's revel are instantly blotted out. The city church that was a dull, deformed, and insignificant building, becomes architecturally beautiful in a pure, clear atmosphere. The warehouse is turned into a palace in the morning light. For the London labourer there is the song of the lark, but it is caged and hung on a nail outside some upper floor window in a dingy street. He has flowers, but they are on the outskirts of Covent Garden Market. His country is brought up to him by the teams and wagons of the market gardener. His children, if they desire grass and greenery, must pluck it by handfuls through the closed railings of the London squares, or dig it up between the stones of unfrequented courts.

When the farmer is at length aroused, and opens his bedroom window to give the orders for the day, he finds the labourers in a tolerably contented condition. To begin with, the weather has at last set fair. There is not a cloud in the sky, and no storm-warning out at sea. The men are not likely to lose a day's wage by huddling in barns or under hedges whilst the golden grain is soaking on the ground. Everything looks well for a glorious harvest day. Turkeys and geese are enjoying an animated conversation from either side of the farmyard; cows and horses alike join in a chorus of congratulation for the fine weather. The first bright beams of the sun are glinting on sea and field, throwing into relief the great new rick of this year's wheat already thatched in the yard, and warming the strewn barley on the field slopes that has been soaked by last night's heavy dew. The faintest of faint breezes blows across the land from the cliffs, just shaking the wisps of straw caught by the hedgerows from last night's waggon load, playing with the leaves of the silver limes, and cooling the atmosphere preparatory to a day of tremendous heat. The foreman and the farmer agree that it is a good ripening day. The wheat is already carried and stacked. The oats have been safely got in. But the barley will be all the better for a good day's drying in the sun. So it is decided to leave off "carrying" until the evening, and to proceed with the "cutting" at the most distant corner of the farm, some mile and a half distant inland. Away go the labourers, with the old foreman at their head—a faithful fellow, who has tilled and cultivated the soil "man and boy" for sixty years, and is living now in the same cottage where he was born. He is very learned on the moot question whether it is better to work the land on the "six year shift," or by a more constant rotation of crops; and he and all the others are decidedly of opinion that the land would produce something better than bright poppies and flowery weeds if it were only encouraged a little more, better ploughed, and treated to a richer manure, than from the mere feeding of cattle and sheep. "Why, in my father's time, this very land yielded double as many coombs an acre than it does now." This is the universal complaint. The question of the "harvest wage" is once more discussed as the farm labourers troop along through the village to their work, calling at their various cottages to tell the missis where the children are to be sent with their dinner at midday. The farmers and the men have had an amicable discussion over the harvest wage. True, the men got seven pounds last year, but times are bad and this year it will not run to more than six pounds five—enough for weekly expenses at home and to save the year's rent from in addition, provided the harvest is a short one. But if, as happens in some cases, it is prolonged over four or five weeks, it will be a pinch to keep the family and pay the rent out of the harvest money. However, in our village the men are sensible fellows. To take six pounds five, to believe the masters, and to live on friendly terms with them throughout the year, is better than to sit at home sulkily on strike, to bear the reproaches of the wife and the sad faces of the children, and to live from hand to mouth on the pittance doled out by the union. So the farmer closes his window, and the men in the merry sunlight trudge forward to their work. The field they are to reap to-day lies in a charmingly picturesque district. We pass from the village over a couple of stiles, and through a sloping barley field yet uncut. At the top of the hill is the new village church—there has only been one wedding in it as yet—that has been built out of the *débris* of the old church, pulled down for fear of destruction from the falling cliff. The church, from which the gloss of newness has not yet worn off, lies in a little nest of romantic farms. What a picture this one would make, with its face of deep green ivy covering and hiding every brick and stone, and its little white gothic windows of lattice work; and this old Eagle Farm is comfortable enough, and splendidly built in the old strong fashion, deriving its name from a sculptured eagle in an embrasure of one of the farm barns. All these hospitable farmers have opened their houses to visitors this summer time. Quiet, dreamy folks they must be, for I seldom see them in my walks, I never find them in the morning bathing on the beach, or at night, when the moon shines over the forgotten dead in the old churchyard. I presume that, although they sleep at night in the old farmhouses, they spend their days for the most part on Cromer sands or on Mundesley beach, driving in at early morning and back at late night. If so, they little understand the charm of farmhouse existence by the sea. They would be happier, if they only knew it, on the cliff and in the cornfields, reading up some forgotten chapter from the exhaustless book of Nature.

The romance of the reaping field departed altogether with the abandonment of the sickle and the scythe. It is only on sloping hills or on uneven ground that the crops are attacked by manual labour. The "click click" of the reaping machine is heard in every field and on every farm. The labourer no longer straightens his bent back when a stranger comes into the field and lays aside his reaping hook for a chat; he dismounts from a kind of chariot, yoked with horses, that tears through the corn and lowers it just as the old war car used to scatter the enemies of Greece and Troy. And I am candidly bound to admit that with the advance of science the reaping machine gets uglier and uglier every year. The "Inventories" has given convenience, but it has discarded beauty. Last year the farmers round about our village used a machine that was, to a certain extent, pretty and graceful enough. A farm lad in a scarlet wideawake and with a skin as brown as a berry rode the leading horse, and a labourer sat on a seat behind emptying the machine of the cut corn as it passed along the ranks, and cast the prostrate wheat in rows upon the ground. But all that is done away with. The newest reaping machine that hails from America is an animated windmill of rakes, that can be worked by a simple farm lad, without any other assistance. He merely sits still and drives the team, whilst the machine, once set going, cuts, collects, and distributes with perfect regularity and order. The field of standing corn is lowered in less than no time, the fallen grain is distributed in even layers, and all that has to be done is to bind it into sheaves and to cart it homeward to the farm.

But for all that, the fun of the harvest-field is not quite at an end, though reaping-machines have taken the place of reapers. The standing corn yields rabbits, and the rabbits in the corn are the perquisites of the reapers—if they can catch them. I fear that rabbit-hunting considerably interferes with the labour of the day. I strolled into a field where they were supposed to be busily cutting, and found, instead of work, an animated chase. The click of the reaping-machine had stopped, the team stood still, the windmill arms were suspended in mid-air, the horses were left to take care of themselves, for the driver, the binder, and half-a-dozen children with sticks and stones were pursuing a rabbit that had been turned out of the corn. Backwards and forwards they chased it, in and out of the corn and across the furrows. They screamed and shouted; but the rabbit was too sharp for its pursuers, and bounded over a hedge right under the nose of a little terrier dog, who got terribly excited, but ultimately lost his head when he was most wanted. These rabbit-hunts occur periodically throughout the day, and they are never carried on with such eagerness as during the hour when the children from the village have brought up to their fathers and brothers the midday meal and a bottle of cold tea, loitering by the way to gather wild flowers or to hunt for the first blackberries in the hedge. Up come the children from the cottages, each with a tin of something good in their hands for father, frightening the partridges from the gorse and fern at the roadside, and driving them to their last refuge this year in the standing barley, or to the turnips from which they will be scared next week and fall to the sportsman's gun. The men in the harvest-field are commendably sober, for the very good reason that they can get nothing strong to drink. In an area of four square miles I have only discovered one solitary public-house, so there is no means whatever of getting malt liquor. Luckily for the reapers themselves, however much they may boast those same "*dura ilia messorum*," as husbandmen did in the days of Horace, their wives are not allowed by the

In the harvest-field—*p.* 52.

Excise to brew "small beer"—detestable stuff at the best; so, like sensible fellows, they fall back upon cold tea, which they drink in profusion. The best presents to distribute at harvest time are tobacco and tea. The men will bless you for one and the women for the other. Both bring eventual peace.

And so the harvest day wears on. The sun gets fiercer and fiercer, and eventually dies down exhausted. The little children, with their empty cans, wend their way homewards. The weary men look to the west, and wonder how long the day will last. How true it is that the "low light gives the colour." The gold of the corn, the green of the fern, the yellow of the hedge daisies, the bright purple of the thistles over which the bees are still busy, are all intensified now that the sun turns red and gradually sinks, a ball of ruddy fire, behind the village church and the old buildings of the silent farm. The reapers are still at work, the thatchers are busy in the glorious sunset, the wagons, laden with the spoils of the fields, are passing from field to farm. But the day is not nearly over. The picture is not yet complete. What remains to be said must be told when the sun has set, by the light of the "harvest moon."

A Harvest Moon.

GLEANING has gone out of fashion. I cannot speak from experience of the customs of other countries, but in this quiet corner of secluded East Anglia gleaning is either too much trouble or it does not pay. Before the reaping machine came into fashion and the silence of the country-side was disturbed with the monotonous "click" of the whirling rakes, and the steady beat of the steam engine in the rick-yard, all these boys and girls released from school and idling under the hedgerows would have been, when the sun was sinking in the harvest field, filling their print aprons or pinafores with such straw and grain as had been left when the last waggon wended its way out of the field, and bore its load to the cosy corner of the big farm. My old friend the miller tells me that when gleaning was the fashion, and the cottagers were industrious, they used to bring him up enough corn and barley to grind as would make a considerable reduction in the household expenses. Many and many a home-made loaf of bread was the result of that pleasant labour in the harvest-field, when the fierce sun had sunk at the close of a lovely summer's day. But all this is over now. Modern machinery sweeps cleaner than the newest of new brooms, and when the little children with their quick fingers, and their mothers with their capacious aprons, are turned into the harvest field to "gather up the fragments that remain, that nothing be lost," they discover no more than can make a satisfactory meal for the farmer's poultry. The cocks and hens, the Michaelmas geese, and the Christmas turkeys are the only gleaners left in these days of modern machinery, so the children are reduced to beg for "largesse" from the passers by, or play "chuck-penny" under the leafy hedges, instead of gleaning; whilst the industrious mothers, whose sunny faces and pink aprons made such an important feature in the English landscapes of William Collins and Birket Foster, find it more profitable to do a bit of washing for the visitors at the Rectory Cottage, or more gratefully obtain a day's labour at the big house. The only gleaner I have seen as yet was an old woman walking home in the heat of the day from the village shop, where they sell everything, from sides of bacon to Balmoral boots, from crewel-worked aprons to apricot jam, who employed her time in relieving the wayside hedges of the wisps of corn that the holly and the hawthorn and the young oak had caught when the laden waggon tottered along from field to farm. But for all that I have a shrewd suspicion that no grain from this unauthorised gleaning will find its way to the windmill overlooking the sea, but will provide a convenient meal for the poultry that cluck outside the cottage gay with gaudy sunflowers, or be consigned to the omnivorous pigs who grunt contentedly in the sty at the back of the lowly cottage.

A harvest field never looks prettier than in the setting sun. When the day is nearly over, and the fierce heat is at an end, the lover of all that is picturesque in nature can revel in the fantastic tricks of colour and light. A pale primrose background is given to the harvest field. The hedgerows, the trees, the ricks nearing completion, stand out in relief against a wall of pure light gold. Every thicket and spinney, each belt of fir-trees helps the effect of a lovely summer sunset. When the sun is high in the heavens that deep green belt of trees round the Rookery Farm, the clump of oak or silver lime that shelters the neighbouring homestead has no special significance. We see the trees, but scarcely notice them. All is different when the sun is setting. The sinking orb finds its delight in darting its varied colours through the branches of the trees that surround an old gabled farm or manor-house. Each day by the careful observer some new effect of sunset may be noticed with delight. On the lighthouse cliff at Cromer, looking west over the little fisher town, a mere cluster of cottages that encircle a tall church tower, the setting sun reddens and burns, and lingers momentarily over the horizon until at last it sinks contentedly into the silent sea; in the quiet graveyard of the old church tower, where a sunset must yield the palm and the poetry to the moonlight, the full effect of the colour is often interfered with by the dazzling lamp of the lighthouse, which contrasts with its bright artificial beams against the multitudinous colours of the dying day. But for the perfection of a sunset you must have trees. At the Rookery Farm, girt round as it is with trees hundreds of years old, in this exquisitely peaceful enclosure, where the barns and farm buildings bear a date when Charles the Second was King of England and where in the ruined farm-house I recently inspected a "priest's hole" only recently discovered by peering down the unthatched roof, the sunset behind the encircling trees assumes a pale blue tone. The best place to see a blue sunset is at the Rookery Farm. I point out its striking beauties to an unimaginative carter who is stabling his horses after carrying the corn, but he can see nothing strange or wonderful in the sight. He is most anxious just now about the bread-and-cheese he will get for supper after his day's labour, and the sleep that is in store for him before he is called at daybreak. What should he care about sunsets, be they blue, or pink, or scarlet? He lives in the only habitable corner of the Rookery Farm that has been saved from ruin, contentedly occupying a haunted house that was once possessed by some yeoman devoted to the King's cause, who may have hidden here many a cavalier; he knows little about pictures or politics, he looks after his horses all day, sleeps well at night, and goes to the village church on Sunday. He has a vote, and owns that it is perfectly useless to him at present. He marvels at the enthusiasm of the chance visitors to his secluded corner of the world, who have in winter time found the first snowdrops at the foot of the rookery trees, who have rifled his hedges and meadows for primroses later on, and who stand now almost awestruck by the silence, leaning over a gate of the unreaped cornfield, and seeing a sunset that would stir the soul of a painter were imagination as profitable an investment in art as it was when Frederick Walker and George Mason told us of the country, and Burlington House was not a gallery of fashionable portraits or a nursery for artists' babies.

A sunset in August forms the proper background for the harvest picture. For the harvest men do not strike work directly the sun goes down. As the sun is creeping down among the trees, or sinking behind the hills, the thatcher, standing out against the faint yellow sky-line, is working on the new-made rick; the reaper in the fields where the machine cannot travel manages to appear on the top of a hillock, so as to make his bent form visible in the golden light; the labourers going home from their work are outlined against the sky, and there is not a feature on the face of nature that is not emphasised at this delightful evening hour. But, best of all, now that the day is ending and the landscape is so still, the pale and quiet harvest moon rises, undefined and indistinct as yet, over the sea cut by the old church tower on the cliff. As the sun sinks lower and lower yet, the pale moon becomes more transparent in the gloaming light. There is a short interval of silence—deep, profound, and exquisitively sad. It is between the daylight and the dark; between the darkness and the day. When the sun has gone its influence is still felt. All the heavens are warm with diffused light; all the fields are aglow with half-forgotten glory. Too brief is the interval of fading light. Then comes the turn of the moon. From extreme pallor it becomes blood red. Then it turns into soft gold, and casts all objects into shadow. The hedges on either side of the leafy lane, the sunflowers and marigolds in the cottagers' gardens, the figures of the people walking homewards are repeated in shadow. Palings and gates are reflected always in shadow in the light of the moon. How chilly it has become already now the sun has sunk! It is more like an October night than a harvest evening in August. A song from a cheerful labourer is heard across the fields in the exquisite silence of the evening. He chants merrily, but still in a minor key, this refrain—"Don't forget your mother when her hair turns grey."

It has a weird and impressive effect, this labourer's song, now that the birds are all at rest, and only whirling bats and solitary owls issue from church towers and blunder about the old farm buildings. Surely, it cannot be—yes, it is—the first fire, with its warm and cosy rays dancing on the latticed windows of one of the cottages on the roadside. There is always something comforting and cheering in the first fire, whether the summer be over or not. Let us enter. We lift the latch, pass down a pretty garden decorated with flowers, admire an old well with its primitive bucket, and are introduced by an aged custodian into one of those blessings of modern rural life—a village club. The good squire has set apart one of his prettiest cottages for the good of the village community. He has appointed as the custodian of the club, a faithful old labourer who, but for this boon, would be in the workhouse or dependent on the bounty of his friends. Poor old fellow! he is alone in the world now. He lost his "good woman" only last year, the best companion and friend he ever had, and tears course their way down his furrowed cheeks as he goes to a drawer of an inner room and brings out for my inspection one of those simple black-

and-white memorial cards that in this instance records the virtues and the death of the old man's faithful wife. "I shall never be happy again, sir, on this side of the grave," murmurs the poor old fellow as he restores the relic to its hiding-place, and totters back again to the fire, "But God's will be done. I shall go to her; but she will not come back to me." Luckily he is well enough to potter about the newspapers that are provided for the members of the village club. A married daughter comes up every day, to look after the old man and tidy him up a bit, and his great age and authority enforce order at night-time when the village lads come up to spell over the paper, to look at the illustrated prints, and to get as much amusement and instruction, as much light and warmth, as they can for the smallest possible subscription.

Of course the village club is better patronised in the long winter nights than in summer time. When harvest is about there is scarcely time to consult the daily or the illustrated weekly papers, to enjoy the simple books of the library, or to play draughts or dominoes. But the little cottage is full to overflowing when the days are short and there is nothing to do from leaving work until the most reasonable bedtime. The only occupant of the village clubroom was an orphan lad that the old custodian had housed out of charity. When I entered, the motherless child was busy playing dominoes by himself, and the old man, just awakened from his afternoon doze in the chimney corner, was engaged in stirring the bright embers of the first autumn fire with his walking-stick. He had much to say and many a yarn to spin about old times and new; but the day was closing fast, and I left them—the old man by the fire, and the lonely little lad at his solitary game—and once more tramped homeward on the road. The moon has risen higher now, and left the sea for the land. How peacefully it shines over the gravestones of the cliff churchyard and lights up the lonely and forgotten tower. Here to this old tower, in winter time, they bring the bodies of the sailors washed up on the shore; and it serves as a village mortuary until the inquest can be held, and they are buried in the far corner of the deserted graveyard. Although the moon is high in the heavens, the silence is so profound, that above the moaning of the sea at the foot of the cliff I can hear the song of the last labourer going homewards by himself or accompanying the latest load of corn to the distant farmyard. Here one might remain for hours—here in this place, at this deserted corner of the world—if it were not for the prosaic pangs of hunger. As I walk through the village in the moonlight and count the lighted windows as I pass, disturbing a dog here, and receiving a cheery "good night, sir," from each labourer at his cottage door, I wonder what the bright-faced "Maid of the Mill," the miller's daughter, who is indefatigable in her care for the stranger, will have to-night for the hungry pedestrian, who has trudged many a mile to-day over cliff, and farm, and field. A dip down through the village, a rise up to the mill, a glimpse of the distant sea, and at last the white palings and the gate, whiter than ever now in the moonlight. How cheerful the pretty house looks, with its one lighted window on the ground floor. The lamps are burning brightly. No gas desecrates this peaceful dwelling, and—capital thought—on this chilly evening for me also there is the first fire burning cheerfully in the wide open grate. Ornaments and shavings are cast aside, and the bright gleam of the fire is cast upon the snowy tablecloth, the silver, and the glass. And what do you say to this for a farmhouse supper, you Sybarites who imagine that nothing can be obtained except at an hotel, with fancy prices and ornamental waiters. A bright red lobster, small and delicate—it was caught this morning under the old church cliffs, and was boiled in the farmhouse kitchen this afternoon, a boiled chicken, also off the estate, and, as a special treat, a blackberry pudding, the fruit gathered from the hedges by the school children in exchange for an occasional "largesse" of pennies. Not bad that for a farmhouse cuisine, the supper washed down by an improvised cup of Apollinaris and Norfolk cider.

And so, after a pipe over the fire, to bed. Not quite yet. Who would shut out, even when it is chilly, so exquisite a night or so beautiful a harvest moon. Open the door that separates the moonlit garden from the quiet household and let us enjoy once more the peace and rest of such a night. The moon has risen to the very top of the sails of the old black mill. It is as light as day. On the other side of the white road the fields of uncut barley stand out against the hills of fern in the clear, pure moonlight. All the flowers are closed and asleep except the evening primrose, that shines forth like a star among the dew-covered roses. The apples on the young trees are reflected in shadow on the garden path. Do holiday-seekers elsewhere find anything much better than this—anything purer or more peaceful—though they journey to the nightless regions of Norway or to the still mountain homes of Switzerland. The sea continues its ceaseless moaning, the revolving lamp on the lighthouse tower casts a pathway of bright gold over the fields. Nature is at rest in the silence that is deeply felt. We are in the harvest fields of England, and "there is no place like home."

"Omnivorous pigs"—*p.* 56.

A Harvest Thanksgiving.

WHEN the ricks are thatched and the labour money paid down, to the delight of the village there comes the time for harvest homes and rural flower festivals. In many a parish and hamlet throughout the width and breadth of England there is held somewhere about the last week of September what is locally known as a dedication service at the old church. The harvest in East Anglia is over, the gleaners have left the field, the threshing machine has been passed on in regular routine from farm to farm; already the plough has turned up the soil carpeted with grass and short stubble; but there remains yet, as a clear and obvious duty, the task of going to church in order to offer up thanks for the mercy of a rich store. On such occasions no difficulties occur in the matter of ritual sufficient to agitate the breast of the most scrupulous churchwarden. At his peril an innovating vicar might propose to light the altar candlesticks, turn to the East at the Creed, wear a fair white linen surplice instead of a black gown, or incline his head at the Doxology. These might be grave matters for the ultimate consideration of ecclesiastical lawyers, and for the weighty decision of Lord Penzance. But hitherto the ceremonies observed at church dedication festivals for the harvest, whether Pagan or not, have escaped the terrors of ecclesiastical contention. They may be as old as the hills; and it is even possible that the ancient deities were approached with just the same simple gifts we observe to-day piled on the communion table and scattered about the aisles of many a little English church. Sheaves of corn, garlands of poppies and corn-flowers, gigantic mangolds, and loaves of bread already made from this year's wheat are reverently placed where they may be typical of the blessings of a rich harvest. They are not considered either idolatrous or impious, and with the strict sanction of pastors and masters the simple labourers all contribute to the decoration, and on this occasion humbly enter the sacred building instead of leaning idly over the old church wall. It is an occasion of some moment. The ordinary sleepy service at three o'clock on the Sunday afternoon is altered to later on in the evening. A brother clergyman from some outlying district is engaged to preach the sermon, the rough wooden pews are lighted with candles, and all concerned in the ingathering of the harvest join heart and voice in an appropriate hymn given out from the harmonium in the chancel. Seldom has late autumn shone upon English rustic life with more beauty than on the year that is now passing away. Londoners who returned home some weeks ago have no idea of the mellow glow of these last days of an unbroken sunshine, for London gets its chill long before it settles on the country. Excursion trains have been specially continued on the time-tables, boats have continued to run that would otherwise have ceased, seaside places show no sign of the close of the season ; for who, unless absolutely compelled, would forego the pleasure of a ramble over cleared fields and amidst hedges of blackberry, or would miss these bright and sunny days and nights made glorious by the hunter's moon ?

Such a sunny September as English farm life often enjoys is specially valuable to the country gentleman released from political duties and anxious to dwell amongst his own people. The squire and the landlord have a great field before them if they only know how to set about the work, and those who have a disposition to be loved, not in a servile, self-seeking fashion, but for the good that is in them, and the sympathies they enlist, will find the best answer to this natural sentiment amongst the simple folk who are not yet inoculated with the feverish independence of those who dwell in towns. The days of Sir Roger de Coverley and old English landlords of that pattern are over and can never be revived. Even the agricultural labourer has his trades union, and is quite as strong in his political as in his religious faith. He votes which way he likes; he elects to go to church or chapel exactly as his conscience directs him. But for all that the tiller of the soil and the husbandman, who earns his daily bread in the open air and in full view of Nature's beauty and beneficence, the woman who works in her little cottage with a flower garden in front of it and the downs and hills for a background have not in any way lost that old-fashioned respect for the squire and his family, the lord of the manor on which they and their ancestors have held cottages for centuries, the master who relieves them when they are sick and sympathises with them in their trouble, or for the ladies who, with gentle sympathy and good breeding, come and make themselves at home with their husbands' and fathers' tenants. Thus it is that harvest sermons at church and harvest suppers in the old barn, with country songs, toasts, and rustic cheers tend to bind together those whose interests are identical, and make good fellowship the closing scene of days of grave anxiety and trouble. The harvest-home and the village flower-show are the pretty ceremonies set apart for an English September. In countries where the vine is cultivated the people are now in the full tide of their autumn merriment, gathering the fruit, treading the winepress, singing their simple songs, working with light hearts and bearing at the close of the vintage bouquets of fresh flowers to the ladies connected with the wine farm. At home, where the corn is grown, the ceremonies are pretty much in the same key, with the addition of flower shows, promoted in order to encourage a healthy competition amongst the owners of those cottage-gardens which are the delight of our incomparable English landscape and the bright spot in our pictures of still life at home. A well-known politician, talking the other day on his estate in Sussex, in his pleasant fashion, had a word to say about flowers as well as crops. He noticed, with some concern, that the offer of prizes for the best-cultivated garden did not meet with the success which had been expected, and then related his own personal experiences as an illustration of his text. "As I grow older," said this venerable man, "I love the flowers more and more. When I was younger I used to like the hills, fields, and woods, and far-off scenery; but now the hills seem steeper and longer than they used to be. But the flowers are always at our feet, and I would therefore commend them for your cultivation and ultimate delight."

It does not need to be a close disciple of Wordsworth, or any one of the poets who intimately study Nature, to feel the truth of these simple utterances of a kindly gentleman bred up in the country, and loving it even beyond the duties which summon him from the woods and fields. This is an age of luxury in flowers as in everything else. The wealthy have their acres of glass and their priceless treasures of exotics and orchids, brought home from the furthest corner of the world; skilled gardeners intermarry the flowers, and produce rare results in colour and form; some cultivate blossoms, and some go mad on variegated leaves; rose bushes and azaleas are artificially trained so as to show all bloom and no leaf; eccentricity of the wildest kind prevails in the conservatory and hothouse. Nor is it different on the sunny slopes of tbe Italian garden, where carpet beds are the latest fashion, where colour is precisely arranged in patches and stripes, and Flora is entrapped into the imitation of the looms of Kidderminster and Wilton, or follows closely the formal lines of architectural design and regular frieze. All these things are curious and no doubt often very beautiful, but can they really compare with the wild luxuriance and fantastic charm of ever-lovable Nature? The leafless wood with its first-spilt cream clots of early primrose; the half cleared thicket carpeted with a rich abundance of heaven blue hyacinth; the quiet village lane starred with the pinky hedge rose and clustering honeysuckle; the treeless down brushed with the colour of the tender and fragile harebell; the wild moorland gay with the nodding bells of tbe crimson foxglove, all musical with the hum of innumerable bees; the yellowing cornfields relieved with the bold scarlet of the poppy and the delicious blue of the wheatflower; the cliff's edge fringed with a mass of tints thrown there recklessly by the prodigal hand of summer; the autumn woods lavish with the glory of their ripe fruits and berries; the groves of mountain ash with their red rosaries pendant from their boughs—these are the handiwork of Nature! And, after all, is not Art powerless in its effort to beat Nature at her own work? What conservatory in the world can give us half the beauty which is contained in the garden of the country, to which the whole world has free admittance? If we desire the contrast direct and immediate, it is ready to our hand. Visitors to the last Paris Exhibition will remember that side by side with the artificial beds of flowers was a grand triumph of disorder, a bed into which seeds and plants had been flung in reckless profusion, allowing colour and form to struggle for the mastery. Nature was permitted to have her way, and Nature put art to the blush. A more beautiful bed of wild flowers was never seen. The gardener at Hampton Court Palace grounds has done something of the same kind, and side by side with his carpet beds, which look as if they had been embroidered with silk, has allowed geraniums, and pansies, and lilies, and rose bushes to grow pretty much at random. The independent flower beds carry off the palm, and Nature once more prevails. It must be remembered, also, that one great feature of these country flower shows is the encouragement given to the culture of the domestic flowers which never lose their charm or the power of their perfume. The grand old cabbage rose, the "double stock with homely cottage smell," the sweet william, the sprig of sweetbriar, and the garnishing of southern wood or familiar "old man," the tufted scabious and the brilliant marigold should not be allowed to die out for want of cultivation. Even the splendid sunflower will outlive the ridicule brought upon it by modern mountebanks, and, together with the evening primrose, the glorious dahlia, and the gay chrysanthemum, make up a wealth of colour to decorate the sunny grave of the dying year.

A pleasant picture.

A Village on the Cliff.

AFTER many wanderings in search of the picturesque, one fine morning I happily alighted on what may fairly be considered a charming watering-place. Concerning the beau-ideal of seaside resorts opinions may no doubt differ. Cromer is not certainly the kind of place one would recommend to the young ladies with travelling trunks filled with fashionable gowns, or to the young gentlemen who consider they are irresistible in blue serge or shepherd's plaid; it is not a paradise for dressing or dancing; its pier or jetty, very limited in extent, affords little opportunity for those exercises of observation and satire which are the prominent amusements of some watering-places. For music Cromer has to depend upon wandering minstrels who have tramped along the pretty Norfolk roads to pipe or grind the airs of Franz Abt and Kucken in the romantic streets of an old-fashioned fishing village. For entertainment it can honestly offer nothing better than the travelling circus that has pitched on a grass meadow within a dozen yards of the grassy cliff overhanging our picturesque and secluded beach. Not a whisper of a music-hall song, not a whistle from the tuneful lips of our familiar friend 'Arry, not a donkey-boy or a goat chaise, not a gipsy or a mountebank, no reciters of poetry on the sands, or advocates of temperance on the shingle, break in upon the consistent peace, the undisturbed quiet of a spot that has the cleanliness of Cornwall, the seclusion of Etretat, the romantic surroundings of Lynton or Ilfracombe, and an air so pure, so bracing, so energising, and so health-giving that it almost makes one break faith with our own familiar Margate and our Westgate-on-Sea of happy memories. It may be safely said, touching the aforesaid idealism of sea-coast haunts, that, as a rule, some strong exception can be taken to almost every popular watering-place round and about our sea-girt islands. One is too shingly, the other too sandy; here the cliffs are too precipitous, there we find no cliffs at all; if the air be charged with ozone and vigour, the landscape, as a rule, is deplorably flat or hopelessly dull; health has to be imbibed with the disagreeable necessity of contemplating barren chalk plains or treeless fields; if, on the other hand, the trees come down to the water's edge, the heather is on the hills, the wild flowers are in abundance, and the neighbouring walks are full of charm and variety, there comes sometimes the disagreeable necessity of feeling that the climate is relaxing, the air moist and humid, and the constitution is diurnally compelled to submit itself to a vapour-bath that leaves the spirits depressed and the frame limp. Judge, then, of my surprise when I stood on the hill that is crowned with the Cromer railway station and looked down on the wooded hollow where the village lies sheltered by two noble sweeps of grassy and fern-covered down. I had left Yarmouth with its stretches of incomparable sand, its unrelieved flatness, its rows of low houses, its long roads, its lakes and dykes, its windmills and Dutch scenery, and had begun to despair of beauty along the Eastern coast. Here, however, was a veritable oasis in the desert, cliffs planted in a district of sandy stretches, woods and groves appearing where no trees had hitherto been seen, the grey square church tower seen in the centre of a cluster of red-roofed houses, a white lighthouse rising from a green garden of

An ideal spot—*p.* 79.

ferns, relieved by bright patches of purple heather, fields covered with scarlet poppy and already ripe for the harvest, flower-fringed lanes, an inexpressible quiet, and above all an air coming across from the sea perfectly laden with vigour, health, and exhilaration. From this overlook at the Cromer Station the village on the cliff was to my mind as bright and bracing as Broadstairs in the old days, with the additional charm of a natural framework of wooded scenery, as prettily situated as leafy Lynton, with the supreme advantage of an aspect straight across the North Sea, whence drive the health-laden breezes. A cynic whispered in my ear as I stood contemplating the distant village, the grassy cliffs, the woods of Cromer Hall in the immediate neighbourhood, the calm blue sea, dotted over with white sails and pleasure-boats, that "the best view of Cromer was to be had from the railway station," and straightway dilated on the tardiness of the speculative builder about the fields and pasture of this ideal spot. He would have cut down the woods and converted them into building plots, carved out the arable land into sites for artistic villas; he would have crowned the grassy cliffs with esplanade and marina, and carted away the fern and the heather to make way for bricks and mortar How differently men view precisely the same situation! Here was I, as I looked down on this romantically-situated and dreamy Cromer, wondering why my countrymen and country-women every summer stuff themselves into the doghole accommodation of such villages as Etretat and Ste. Addresse, paying fabulous sums for accommodation that peasants would despise, submitting themselves to inconveniences and disorder on a shingly beach under an ugly cliff with an uninteresting background, when here was—a fishing village, it is true—but a clean and commodious one, a sand almost as good as Yarmouth, a cliff as smooth as a lawn-tennis plot, and a surrounding country as beautiful and as varied as any that the most favoured districts of England could afford. It was a bit of Devonshire transplanted to the Eastern coast. My more practical friend could not see such a situation at all with my eyes. In imagination he had pulled down Cromer and built it up again on a new model, he had built a row of villas between the lighthouse and the village, and he had covered the span intervening between the railway station and the old grey flint church and its solemn grey tower with a speculative estate, placarded with lodgings and apartments in every other window. I am not at all prepared to say that all this will not be done in a few years time. The eye of the speculative builder is firmly fixed on poor little Cromer. New houses are springing up like mushrooms. The hod and the trowel have advanced as far as Overstrand. For my own part, I prefer the Cromer of the past to the Cromer of the present. Into the future I will not inquire.

If you want to have an idea what Cromer is, how simple its life, how peaceful its little history, how much charm it contains for the recluse and the reading man, what fields for the naturalist and botanist, what butterflies are to be caught there, what ferns to be selected, what sketches to be made at sunrise and sunset, what walks the neighbourhood provides, what mornings on the fern-covered downs looking out to sea, what afternoons amongst the woods of Felbrigg and Sherringham, what lawn tennis on the firm white sand, what evenings on the old wooden pier when the sun is sinking, what nights of sleep, though the wild wind howls out seaward —come with me, and I will try to sketch a Cromer day. The only charm is its simplicity; its only recreation is its rest. For costume you may put on a lawn tennis jacket, some flannels and shoes, and walk about the village streets without being stared at; thus apparelled you may go upwards to the downs or downwards to the sea; for companion you can have nothing better than a book to squeeze under your arm, unless, indeed, fate has bestowed on you a closer and more actual sympathy—a voice to listen to and a mind to share, a face to brighten, and a heart to enjoy. I saw two such sympathetic ones only just now working their way towards the lighthouse cliff, happy in the possession of youth and lightheartedness, facing the breezes, each intent on the other, and I watched them lessening in the distance until they disappeared behind a rising down and were lost to view. They seemed on the whole far happier than the conventional young lady who pretends to read a book on the seaside pier, though she manages to look up undesignedly at every passer-by, or the still more conventional youth, who brings Bond-street airs to the sea and the shingle, and whose sense of enjoyment is derived from the prodigality of starch imparted to his shirt-collar by an admiring laundress. At Cromer, however simple we may be, we are at least natural; and if my plan of a seaside day is considered by many dull and slow, monotonous and uneventful, it may be possibly appreciated by an idle few who do not wholly neglect the pleasures of imagination.

It is morning at Cromer, the sun high in the heavens, a strong north-west wind blowing, the sea just flecked with white, and a good prospect of fair weather at last. The air, coming in fresh to the bedroom window, has already new life in it; no sound is heard above the wind but the fisherman calling lobsters in the streets. Although so early on this bright summer morning, already there is one sight that is missed. From the very window with the sea outlook it might be possible, had not sleep been so strong, to behold a sunrise as beautiful as any that drags the visitors out of their beds on the top of Righi Kulm, in Switzerland. For Cromer, let me tell you, is one of the few watering-places where, in the summer months, you can, from the same window, see the sun rise straight out of the ocean at morning, and the sun disappear in glory of orange and scarlet in the evening. As yet, however, I have noticed no disposition to study sunrises at Cromer. The air is so laden with sleep, the whole district is so covered with poppies, that the four o'clock arousing is, I find, indefinitely postponed. Young ladies leaning upon the Cromer balconies after breakfast make up their minds to see the sun rise the very next morning, but somehow or other their good resolutions fail them, and so far we have had to depend for description of them on the homely Ruskinese of the Cromer fishermen and boatmen, who highly extol the beauties we have lost, with a view, no doubt, to an arrangement whereby a better view of the sunrise might be obtained from the deck of the Maud or the Alice. I must therefore be permitted to pass over the Cromer sunrise as a postponed pleasure, and take you at once to the yellow sands for a morning bath. What a queer, ancient, rambling village it is, reminding one of Cornwall at every turn; the fine old church with the ruined chancel, now being rapidly restored, squeezing itself into a cluster of cottages, and towering over the tiny street. There are not many signs of life, although the clock has struck eight. The fruit and flowers, great peaches and purple grapes, plums and gooseberries, bunches of roses, and bundles of sweet pea are coming in from the country in the village carts; at the lifeboat station they are adjusting the barometrical chart, and the keeper of it, looking at the falling mercury, promises only doubtfully a fine day; the coastguardmen outside their neat cottages, standing on their smooth patch of lawn, are occupied as usual with looking out to sea at apparently nothing, but with a most determined purpose; at the corner of every street is a bronzed and healthy-faced sailor with a knowing look in his face which implies that it is the best possible day for a sail or a fishing expedition; the children are already on their way to the sands with their spades and buckets; but the bathers are the most important factors in the nomadic population. It is the best way to the bath to go by the cliff, and then down a sandy staircase—for the faculty recommend an air bath as well as a sea bath at Cromer, and I cannot conceive a better one than can be found on the height round by the coastguard station. And a fresher dip it would be difficult to find, whether from a boat out at sea or from a machine on the beach. It is not too rough nor too calm, and with a brisk walk home by the sands or the cliff the jaded Londoner can put on such an appetite as will astonish his landlady and increase materially the sale of Cromer shell fish.

Breakfast over there is only one thing more to

be done, a walk on the sands and so onwards to the cliff. But sand life at Cromer is not like sand life elsewhere. There is plenty of amusement, but very little noise. On Bank Holiday there are a few swings and roundabouts, but now we have relapsed into our normal decorum and propriety. The nigger and the music-hall minstrel never desert Yarmouth for its quieter neighbour ; a photographer, it is true, pursues his silent trade, but, as a rule, the visitors provide amusement for themselves. The young ladies bathe, of course, and display a wealth of uncombed back hair ; different families are distinguished by their domestic tents pitched on the sands, as at Boulogne and elsewhere ; lawn tennis parties abound, for the sands are hard and firm, and it is surprising with what devotion enthusiastic admirers of the game will drag nets, poles, and paraphernalia from their cliff lodgings to some selected spot miles away across the sand. Peace and comfort reign supreme. Some sketch, others read, more geologise. The children seem fonder of hunting for crabs and sea anemones than of building pyramids and Mont Cenis tunnels. They do not cramp themselves into a given circle, as elsewhere, but, as the beach is wide and safe, they scatter to Overstrand in one direction and towards Sherringham in the other, paddling as children will do, and shortening the hours by wearing out their shoes and flinging smooth pebbles into the sea.

But enough of the sand, however amusing; the sailing yachts have gone out, under the guardianship of the honest sailors, who have enough to do with their lifeboat in winter time; the Yarmouth steamer has arrived, and as the weather is fair has been met and unloaded by the beach-boats; the children are scattered, and the sands are tiring, so let us mount at once to the cliffs up there by the white lighthouse, which is so prominent a feature in the landscape. This is, perhaps, the best spot in all Cromer. They say that the Cromer cliffs are gradually falling away, that the sea has registered a vow to make an end of this charming little village; landslips after landslips have given their customary warning, and scarce a winter passes without some arable acres falling into the hungry ocean. Indeed the inhabitants, to preserve their houses over their heads, have been compelled to fortify the village with strong sea walls, fearing lest red-roofed street, grey church and all, should one day topple over into the sand, and Cromer be a matter of history. It is for this purpose that the latest lighthouse has been erected, far back on the Cromer grass cliffs, lest it should fall, as did its immediate predecessors, into the sea. Once mounted to the Lighthouse Point, Cromer may be viewed at its very best. The cliffs for miles round are covered with an under-growth of fern and heather, divided by green paths as firm and true as a billiard table. No glaring white is to be seen anywhere ; the cliffs are brown and sandy, the sea blue, the landscape of a universal green. Once up here you can wander for miles along the cliff in peace and quiet, amongst farms and cornfields, and such a variety of wild flowers as I have rarely seen collected together. The brilliant scarlet of the poppy, growing not only in the cornfield, but in masses and borderings at the cliff's edge ; the bright gold of the wild yellow tulip, an inhabitant of these favourite districts ; the deep mauve of the Scotch thistle, and the constant purple of the heather make Cromer cliffs a veritable flower garden—a rare accessory to any English seaside place. On these cliffs, never deserted by a breeze, surrounded by scenery so rich and varied with farm land and wood on the right hand and the uncomplaining sea on the left, it would be strange indeed if a luxurious morning could not well be spent, a morning of that idleness which is no stranger to reflection or imagination. Here, resting on the cliff amongst the wild flowers, the blue sky overhead, the air exhilarating, the martins and swallows darting from their holes in pursuit of insects, the corn waving as the breezes sweep across the fields, the sea face chequered with purple and blue as the clouds flit over the surface, away from the madding crowd, from noise and din and discord and vulgarity, seems the place where busy brains and tired frames might rest for a while and be at peace.

"Facing the breezes"—*p.* 82.

Comfortable Cromer.

I LEFT the good people of Cromer, if you remember, after describing a healthy and invigorating village on the cliff, busily occupied in those careless pleasures which are apparently inseparable from the seaside. For it must not be imagined, although we have no representative brass band, no rotunda on the pier-head, no fashionable promenade, no evening dances, no assembly rooms, and very few opportunities for social intercourse, that we scorn the childlike amusements which spring at once from contentment and seclusion. On the contrary, I should say that it would be difficult to find any place of the kind where the visitors who have arrived at a mature and sensible age are more ready to revert to the innocent pleasures of their infancy. Cromer is certainly not distinguished for its children—that is to say they bear a very slight percentage to the total of its inhabitants. It may be that the sandy and shifting cliffs, with

"Cromer Sands"—*p.* 90.

their ugly gaps and ravines, their crumbling bases and tottering cornices, frighten the hearts of nervous mothers; it may be that the necessarily limited accommodation of the village, its fisherman's cottages and doll's-house little rooms, alarm the mind of paterfamilias, who, with the best intentions in the world, may be excused for hesitating before he shuts himself up in a bandbox for a month with the olive branches watered by the salt sea and invigorated by the air. To tell the truth, the weather is not, on the whole, more constant at Cromer than elsewhere; for one sunny day, when outdoor exercise can be taken from morning until night, we have to endure clouds and wind, thunder and showers, and, it is surely unnecessary to add, a wet day at the seaside is considerably aggravated in its woe by the immediate companionship of children made wild by the atmosphere, and unamenable to all discipline in consequence of the freedom that they, like their elders, are so apt to misconstrue and abuse. The children at Cromer, so far as I have observed, are all good children. There are few babies and bottles. The sands are not turned into a nursery. Thus far I have not seen a perambulator or a goat-chaise. At Yarmouth the babies swarm between one jetty and the other. Holes and hollows are dug in the sands, and down into it the miserable infant is plunged, with a feeding-bottle in its mouth, whilst the nursemaid turns aside and flirts with the photographer's assistant. Rations are served out at Yarmouth by the head nurse, seemingly most appetising to the hungry family, although they consist of sanded bread-and-butter or scraps of bread and cheese produced from a reticule. We see no such exercises of domestic care at Cromer. The boys all look as if they were home from a public school, had read Cæsar's Commentaries, and were thinking of starting next term on the Iliad of Homer. They are well-made, active lads, very busy with their butterfly-nets on the Light-house cliff, amongst the ferny undergrowth, and organise exploring parties for sea anemones on the rocks when the tide is low. Apparently these bright-eyed and well-behaved young gentlemen are candidates for some science prize which will be competed for when the school meets again after the holidays. A short story, founded on fact, will illustrate the conduct of the Cromer lad as contrasted with the noisy youth who makes life hideous at most seaside places. The other afternoon I was astonished to find a young, well-built and generous-looking English lad careering along the narrow streets of the Cromer village, holding a fisher urchin by the ear and keeping him fast, notwithstanding his fitful shrieks. It appears that there had been a kind of "town and gown" row between the Cromer youngsters and the public schoolboy visitors, and that one of these young scamps had, in a cowardly fashion, hurled a stone and hit the visitor on the forehead. Smarting with pain, the lad refused to thrash his insignificant assailant, who was smaller than himself by many inches, but with stern justice took him by the ear, saying, "I can't thrash you, you little beggar, you are so beastly small; but I will take you to your father, and he shall do it for me."

In the absence, then, of children at Cromer, those of mature age are not indifferent to the childlike amusements of the sands wherever they are found. These consist of digging and paddling. Fortifications, ramparts, and architectural designs of great elaboration are daily created, by the curate or the tutor, for a reading party of mixed sexes, and I have my eyes to bear me witness that in the case of young and beautiful ladies no years of discretion remove an inherited taste for what is popularly known as "paddling." Paddling, I need scarcely observe, consists of skirting the fringe or margin of the sea with naked feet, and the pleasure is derived from watching the wavelets at low tide break upon the lower extremities, relieved from the encumbrance of shoes and stockings. This occupation is, as a rule, confined to children properly equipped for the occasion; but Cromer is at once so quiet and innocent in its habits that it is no unknown thing for a lonely pedestrian on the sands to come across a party of nymphs, true to their Venus-born origin, surprised at their partial ablutions by some wandering Actæon with no curiosity whatever in his composition. But come with me, now that the luncheon-bells are ringing at all the little inns and boarding-houses, and see of what Cromer society is composed. We will stand at the head of the cliff staircase by the coast-guard station, for here all Cromer must pass on the way to those lobsters awaiting them on the hospitable board. It is a very charming and select society. Boys in flannels and striped cricket-caps come with their butterfly-nets from happy hunting-grounds within a good square mile of the lighthouse hill; girls and maidens in fantastic costumes, bright-eyed, active, and full of

"Paddling Nymphs"—*p.* 94.

health, troop in from the cliffs and country lanes about Overstrand with sheaves of fern and wild flowers under their arms; young fellows, very probably in the first eleven at some public school, toil across the sand and up the steps towards home burdened with lawn-tennis nets, and followed half wearily by disappointed or successful players; mermaidens with hair streaming down their backs mount to the cliff freshened from the bath; up they come from fishing, from sailing, from exploring, from paddling, from dozing, and from dreaming, and they are followed presently by the really studious with a volume of Ruskin in the pocket or a life of Goethe under the arm, and are joined by a whole army of intelligent young ladies, who, with sketch-books and easels, turn out Cromer beeches, Cromer mornings, Cromer nooks, Cromer caves, and Cromer sunsets as rapidly as the copyists in Continental picture-galleries.

But how few seaside places there are where mornings on the sands and on the cliffs can be varied in the afternoon by picturesque rambles in a district especially favoured for its flower-land and foliage. At the seaside elsewhere after luncheon it can fairly be said that "all that can be has been done." It must always seem the same thing over again; the same sands, the same sea, the same cliffs, the same amusements, the same faces. How few holiday haunts there are where the beach and the boats are not backed by a flat chalky pasture or a treeless desert. People are planted on the sands, and there they must stay. Not so, however, at Cromer. Apart from a country containing almost every possible variety of English scenery, with here a bit of Exmoor and there a scrap of Cornwall; irrespective of the quiet and romantic farms nestling in wood and shrubbery within sound of the sea and of the breeze; of the heather-covered heaths and commons; of the country cottages with their homely, old-fashioned, English flowers, as sweet now as in the days of Shakespeare; of the lanes and roads, bordered on either side by thicket and wood, full of ground game and singing birds, and playing places for the lively squirrel; apart from a district in which there is never any glare, and ever present a sense of farmland and greenery, we have in the immediate neighbourhood of Cromer estates and parks whose beautiful acres are every week placed at the disposal of the public by their liberal and generous-minded owners. There is Cromer Hall, within a stone's-throw of the village; there is the well-known estate of Felbrigg, recalling the dismal story of the last Wyndham owner, who ruined a princely inheritance in hideous dissipation and wild riot, the Wyndham of everlasting memory, who entertained prizefighters as his boon companions at the hall, and drove his horses to death gallop-ing a coach between Norwich and Cromer. There is the beautiful park of Mr. Upcher at Sherringham, and there is Lord Suffield's place at Gunton, all thrown open to the public on certain days with a liberality that extends to free access even up to the drawing-room windows. This is, of course, no slight privilege. In variety of foliage and richness of colour these estates, with their parks and shrubberies, are as remarkable as such show places as Tregedna, near Falmouth, with the additional advantage of an air charged with tone, vigour, and freshness. We have none of the moist atmosphere and relaxing climate of the Cornish lanes and parks, where the ferns grow so luxuriantly and the blue hydrangeas flourish; but at Felbrigg or Sherringham the heather blooms and the beeches wave, and the lovely silver pine, with its greenish-blue tassels, sighs all day in an air that braces nerve and sinew by its strength and its softness. What wonder, then, that all Cromer goes into the heart of the country on these welcome summer afternoons, delighted to vary the sea and shore with inland scenery from which the sea is never absent. There is little need for horses or carriages, for all these show places are within an easy walk of Cromer; but still, throughout the afternoon, the little pony traps with their scarlet jockeys, modelled after the Scarborough plan, drive up to that bit of Exmoor-like scenery at Beeston, where on an eminence said to be a Roman encampment, but more probably an old beacon station, may be viewed the fairest prospect of distant sea and near foliage that ever delighted the picturesque sense.

But there is one sight left before the evening closes in and before, "with stars and sea winds in her raiment, night sinks on the sea." That sight is a Cromer sunset. The day is almost done, a silvery tone is stealing over the landscape, more silent now than ever; the grey, square tower of the Cromer church stands out clear and distinct over the red roofs of the unpretending little village. The lighthouse cliff is quite deserted; no one wends his way to the grassy paths surrounding the white lighthouse tower, from whose summit a revolving gleam is

"Exmoor-like Scenery"—*p.* 89.

cast upon sea and land. But on the eastern cliff, all who would enjoy a peaceful scene are found walking at the cliff's edge towards Sherringham. There is yet light left for the harrow that is busy in the farm land, and the labourers toil on in the fields in presence of the advancing shadows. "The low light gives the colour." How true this is may be seen from the brilliant scarlet of the poppy in the ripened corn, and from the gay bordering of wild flowers fringing the fields and the cliff. A long line of gold and purple is traced upon the wet sands and the advancing sea. In the far distance a couple of lovers advance towards the fading light. There is no sense of melancholy, although the landscape is so very still. Some adventurous fisher lads are swarming down the sides of precipitous sand cliffs in search of the nests of the sand martins that dart across the cliffs' edge and skim the fields. At Sherringham Point, sitting round an old boat, may be seen a group of bronzed fair-haired fishermen that would be a welcome study for Hook. Lower and lower the sun sinks into the sea, tinging the sky with rose-colour and gold, until at last it is met in its descent by a misty grey cloud, and with one short gleam the light has gone, leaving only a roseate reflection over farm and field. There is little more to be done; the sea alone keeps up its ceaseless moaning; the fields and cliffs look chilly and deserted; people come up from the pier and the esplanade, and when the church clock has struck ten the best part of Cromer is asleep.

"Whirling around in its old-fashioned way"—*p. 27.*

Lazy Lowestoft.

ON a recent journey between Norwich and Lowestoft I was enabled, from the window of a railway carriage, to make still further acquaintance with those silent rivers and sunny "broads" which form such a pleasant feature of the landscape in this delightful district. Now that the Fisheries Commissioners have been to see them, and holiday articles have been written and pictures have appeared in the illustrated papers, perhaps in years to come campers out and canoeists, anglers and yachtsmen, dreamers and painters, smokers and idlers, will come and make acquaintance with the waterways of Norfolk and Suffolk, bordered with trees and pasture land, teeming with fish, and decorated at every turn with waving reeds and wild flowers. The somewhat inevitable comparison to Holland, with its red-roofed houses and constant windmills, its lazy rivers and wind-swept reaches, may, however, prepare the reader for a district striking enough, yet, after all, flat and unprofitable. Believe me, this is not the case if you will only take the train from Norwich to Lowestoft on a sunny September morning, and, discarding the newspaper, look steadily out of the window. One well-remembered day, when I was on board a smart racing yacht bound from Yarmouth to Oulton regatta, when the coy and uncertain wind played such desperate pranks with us, and we sailed with difficulty there and "quanted" so laboriously home, I had time enough to study the main features of the waterscape, to note the churches and the villages, to count the various specimens of birds and wild flowers on the way, to see the heron and to disturb the meditative angler. It did not require very much stretch of imagination to dream of the delightful indolence of a summer's holiday, "pottering" about these canals and lakes, which have their own beauty and more variety of incident than our own Upper Thames contains. For it is no desolate region. There are little inns where you can put up and find cheery companions when sick of the confinement of the yacht's cabin, and many a waterside village and hamlet very well worth exploring. But I had no idea of the beauty of the broads and rivers until I saw them under a September sun later on in the season, when the wind was more favourable for sailing, and fishing had begun in good earnest. Norwich always strikes me as one of the most delightful of provincial cities. It has no suburbs, so to speak. You do not enter the town through grimy outskirts or unpicturesque manufactories, but find the quiet, contemplative river stealing up to the old city walls, a river with idlers on the bank and fishermen on the stream, so intent and earnest on their sport that they do not deign to notice the passing train. The harvesters pay attention to us from their labour in the corn, they pause in their work, wave their hats and handkerchiefs to us; the villagers shout to us as we pass, but the fishermen never stir or make any sign whatever. There they remain wrapt in forgetfulness of the world around them, and nothing wakes them from their reverie. From the elevated position of the railway you can have a wider outlook over these dreamy streams and peaceful rivers. At odd moments you can see half a dozen white sails—and how bright, clear, and white they look against the background of autumn green—of the pleasure yachts tacking from river to broad and from broad to river, and as many more of the deep-red-sailed wherries or flat-bottomed barges sailing indolently along an avenue of waving rushes, with the man at the painted helm smoking the inevitable pipe. None of the pleasant features of English scenery are absent; the cattle grazing in the water meadows, bright birds, church spires, old ruins, quaint inns and pretty villages are all dotted about the pleasant pictures that meet the eye from the time the train glides out of Norwich Station and arrives amidst the same calm and quiet at Lowestoft, which is perhaps the most fashionable and select watering place on this pleasant coast.

I shall always look upon Lowestoft as the very pink of propriety. It is certainly the cleanest, neatest, and most orderly seaside spot at which I have ever cast anchor. There is an air of respectability at the very railway station, no confusion, no touting, no harassing, and no fuss. I am not bothered by hotel porters or omnibus men, or lodging-house keepers or advertisers. When I come to Lowestoft I am expected to know where I am going to, and not to require any further information. I have hardly got into the streets before I discover signs of the same scrupulous order. The shops are prettily arranged, the people are so well disciplined that they always keep in a file to the right or to the left, never running up against or jostling one another on pathway or foot-bridge, and so considerate are the Lowestoft Improvement Commissioners that they actually provide visitors with a wooden summer-house or shelter in case they should be tired or caught in a shower before they arrive on the beach. Literally this is no exaggeration. At convenient corners of the town are erected shelters or rooms provided with tables and benches, where, without paying a farthing, anyone can rest or converse without impeding the traffic. Such shelters as these would be well appreciated in the London suburbs, or on such weary thoroughfares as the Finchley Road or Haverstock Hill, where, with much difficulty, even a bench is found. I perceive that Lowestoft is very regular and precise in its ways, and it would be rank heresy to attempt to modify or alter her customs; but before dwelling on this exactness of holiday life, let me once more call attention to the trim and bandbox appearance of breezy Lowestoft. Not Folkestone, with its Lees, or Sandgate, with its villas, can compete with the Dutch cleanliness, the symmetry, and the precision of this treeless, sunny promenade. Lowestoft, of course, has its pier, not one of those meaningless, lengthy jetties that jut out into the sea and so seriously disfigure the prospect, not a stretch of boards and piles, with a beginning, a middle, and an ending that can be indefinitely prolonged, but a pier that is attached to a harbour, a pier that encloses a basin, a pier with a miniature or toy lighthouse at the end of it, a pier at whose side yachts lie at anchor and from whose steps gaily dressed young ladies start to row or sail these sunny afternoons. Let me be very particular on this point. No one at Lowestoft would dream of going out for a sail until after luncheon. The morning is for the sand, the afternoon for the pier, the sunset for the promenade, and the evening once more for the band and the pier.

Besides the pier, which is a great feature at Lowestoft, though it is scrupulously select, with no refreshment rooms, bazaars, fancy shops, weighing machines, tame owls, performing cats, or phrenologists, there is of course a sea at Lowestoft, and a beach, half pebble and half sand, and in front of all an hotel and a row of houses that look to me as if they had come out of a toy building box from the Lowther Arcade.

Lowestoft Harbour—*p.* 106.

The hotel is a very magnificent and imposing-looking building, immediately facing the pier gates, and then, running along the sea front, we have a row of villas, all of the same pattern, shape, and order. A soft-sanded promenade is faced by a stone balustrade, with seats in circular abutments for the weary; and huge statues, representing Neptune or some marine monster, guard the ends of this most select and respectable colony. I do not think I ever saw so neat a place out of Holland—the place looks as if it were dusted and tidied up every morning, and I secretly believe that if I had dropped the end of a cigar on the faultless esplanade, the Lowestoft Improvement Commissioners would have seized upon me and handed me over to the town bailiff, or some such other mysterious official, for creating disorder and setting an evil example.

When I arrived at Lowestoft it was the period of the day allotted to lolling on the sands and shingle. It was one of the hottest mornings I can remember, with a sunstroke in every glare. The beach is unprotected by cliff, and I should not have thought that the most comfortable place to read a novel was on a bed of pebbles with the head resting on a pillow of shingles covered with a pocket-handkerchief. But no

Lowestoft visitor, notwithstanding the evident discomfort, neglected the obvious duty of attending the sands in the morning. There they all were—the children on the sands, the attendants on the shingle, the old folks watching them from their seats on the stone work of the esplanade. For weeks and weeks they must have been doing exactly the same thing, pitching the same sized stone into the same sea, reading or working in the same uncomfortable attitudes, gathered round the bathing machines and the entertainers, but never stirring from the spot until the luncheon bell rang out from one of the sea-fronted villas, or mamma beckoned to her darlings from the upper balcony to tell them of the readiness of the mid-day meal. A more domestic spot than Lowestoft surely does not exist around the coast of England. I do not think I ever saw more children attached to individual families, or visit a spot where the proud position of being connected with these well-filled quivers was so conspicuously advertised. Elsewhere paterfamilias, amiable enough in his way, is inclined to shirk the responsibility of his position. If he is quite certain that his olive branches are bound for the pier, he will conveniently hie him to the beach; when they are busy with the spade on the sand, he will be snugly ensconced in a corner of the pier with a pipe and a newspaper. Not so, however, at Lowestoft. The man who has his quiver full of them publicly pronounces his happiness. The afternoon pier is the occasion for the great Lowestoft baby show. The band plays, and the infants are trotted out for inspection. You can see that they have all been carefully groomed; the nurse and nursery governess have been diligently at work to remove the traces of the early dinner. Up and down the children walk, with their dolls and toys, between an avenue of delighted and envious parents. There is something very charming, simple, and innocent in this charming arrangement, but it sometimes leads to scenes that were better hidden in the nurseries of the esplanade. When a refractory infant is anxious, nay, determined, to go out for a sail, and its parents have other views on the matter, and when the battle royal between conflicting opinion is only fought out with screams on the one side and slaps on the other, it would appear as if the afternoon pier, with the band playing, was scarcely the place for such practical illustrations of the value of Solomon's proverb. But the good people of Lowestoft do not care, not a bit of it! They are proud of their children and their little tempers. Mamma wheels the latest in the family perambulator, and papa beams behind his book as the refractory child is promptly and efficiently punished. Let it be remembered that these are all middle-class people of the highest respectability; no trippers or excursionists mingle in these domestic rites; the baby who screams is smothered in lace and insertion; the young gentleman who has a difference with his nurse is in a white sailor suit of unexceptional spotlessness. When they have duly exhibited their children—and their respective tempers—listened to the band, gone out for a shilling or sixpenny sail, and duly gossipped on a pier, without shelter and exposed to the fiercest afternoon sun, they all go indoors at the moment when life is beginning to be endurable in the open air. This course is, however, necessary in order to prepare for the most delightful feature of a Lowestoft day—the evening pier, when the babies are in bed, and Lowestoft, select and respectable as it is, can indulge in those harmless reveries, flirtations, and repartees that make seaside life endurable. The band plays merrily from its kiosque in the middle, and strange to say, not at the end of the pier; a breeze springs up from the sea and makes one forget the almost intolerable heat: the yachts and pleasure boats rock in the little harbour; the waves plash up against innumerable keels; backwards and forwards goes the procession in the semi-darkness; some become sentimental, and many more meditative, until, with perfect punctuality, the concert is brought to a close, and, as if by clockwork, all Lowestoft is moved off to an early bed.

A Playground by the Sea.

THE epigrammatic visitor might briefly describe Great Yarmouth as a Rotterdam without its costumes, combined with a Scheveningen without its dulness There is something irresistibly Dutch about this popular watering-place on the East Coast. It is Dutch in its streets, Dutch in its sands, Dutch in its inland scenery. Where else but here and in Holland can you find dykes, broads, canals, and brackish lakes; where else such a collection of sedges, reeds, waterfowl, and windmills as may be discovered by the curious within an easy journey of this playground by the sea? Of the Norfolk and Suffolk broads I shall have something to ask by and bye; we who know and love the East coast often wonder why Thames yachting men and fishermen, naturalists and men of science are not more often found learning how to steer and sail on the Yare or on the Waveney, with topsails gleaming along the

Yarmouth Market Place—*p.* 113.

surface of Braydon Water, or making their way by river, canal, and artificial cutting to Oulton Broad; I shall have to question these campers-out by our favourite Thames river why they know so little of the trip from Yarmouth to Wroxham, or fail to make themselves acquainted with the picturesque scenery of our English Holland, described so well by Wilkie Collins in his admirable novel of "Armadale." For the present, however, my purpose is to deal alone with Yarmouth and Yarmouth proper, with the headquarters of Bloater Land, with the childhood's home of David Copperfield, and the scene of the loves of Steerforth and Little Em'ly, with the birthplace of Peggotty and Ham, and the wailing ground of Mrs. Gummidge, with the city of the old "rows," and the old-fashioned market place, which has somehow lost all its salt, fisherlike, and briny air, and been turned—at least, in summer time—into one of the most marvellous playgrounds of sand that I have ever found round and about these islands of ours. I have mentioned Rotterdam and Scheveningen not without reason. The first impression of a place is everything; it is instantaneously acquired, but it never leaves one. Directly I left the railway station at Yarmouth and drove across the bridge on to the quay, where else could I be in the world but at Rotterdam? The banks of the canal or river planted with trees, the old Norfolk wherries at the quayside, with painted masts and hulls and fantastic pennons; the London steamer just arriving and in process of being moored to the quayside; the foreign-looking Town Hall facing this scene of arrival, departure, and merchandise: the gaiety, variety, and picturesqueness of the place—brought Holland and the Boompjes instantly back to the memory. But a seaside place is not characterised by its railway station, its quays, its market places, or its churches. They may be all very varied, antiquated and interesting, but it is only fair to own that the ordinary run of seaside visitors decide for or against a popular watering-place by its sea front. A man will lose his temper who, going down to the sea, does not get a bedroom immediately facing the ocean. He may sit up half the night in the smoking-room, arise at cock crow, and comfortably sleep in the chamber devoted to that purpose; but it is essential to his happiness that he shall have an outlook seaward. When the family is despatched to its allotted month of sand-digging and paddling half the enjoyment is cut off if the lodgings are in a street running at right angles to the waves instead of facing them. When I first saw the sea front of Yarmouth it was Scheveningen that was recalled. I had pictured the ordinary English watering-places, the tall houses, the monster hotels, the neat gardens and enclosures, the occasional shrubberies and greeneries; I had never conceived a playground by the sea with such little architectural beauty. The Corporation, however, must be congratulated upon the great improvements that have taken place during the last few years, for now the eye is relieved by the charmingly laid-out Beach Gardens, with its well-gravelled walks and judiciously seated concrete promenade, a rough piece of waste land has been transformed by skilful hands, guided by an artistic taste, into one of the most delightful retreats that can be found at any seaside resort. A more magnificent stretch of sand the coast of England cannot produce; so now with the beach to attract the children, and the gardens to delight the worn-out, the jaded, and the depressed, Yarmouth will continue to grow in popular favour and esteem. There is, however, no imposing mansion along the whole of the magnificent coast here. There are few gardens or green trees. The seaside promenade is flat, wide, and uniformly yellow. The seaside lodging-houses are dwarfed villas. Public buildings of a decidedly unromantic character, such as a military depot, a naval hospital, a sailor's home, a cemetery, a workhouse, and a small-pox hospital are permitted to stand out boldly to sea, and to occupy sites that would delight the speculative builder. There is no doubt a small, snug, and select West-end of Yarmouth in the neighbourhood of the Victoria Hotel, where an attempt has been made to vary the monotony of the sandy promenade. The Assembly Rooms stand back in a garden plot, and the houses adjacent boast a frontage of lawn; but at Yarmouth the East-end predominates. The friends of the town are fond of freedom, and do not care to be smart. They must have oyster-stalls on the fashionable promenade; they must have public-houses exposed to the sea; they must have all the means at hand for refreshing and delighting the countless thousands who are poured upon the Yarmouth sands day after day and week after week, from north and south, cockneys and manufacturers, London and Leeds, Dock-Land and Doncaster, by the enterprising railway company which is

Yarmouth Beach—West-end—*p.* 116.

alive to the value of such a stretch of sand. Margate and Ramsgate put together, in the height of the season, could not produce so many children as are found every morning and afternoon on the Yarmouth sands. Not even in the old days, before the London, Chatham, and Dover Railway Company built their station and destroyed the proper meaning of Mr. Frith's picture, did Ramsgate contain one-half of the variety, business, and excitement that are to be found to-day at Yarmouth. To begin with, it is sand of exceptional purity. There are sands elsewhere that are only half sands, sands with streaks of shingle in them, sands with morasses and wet places, with ugly fords to be got over as at Boulogne, sands where lakes spring up at certain tides that wet the summer costumes and disturb the children. Not so at Yarmouth. The sands here are like the finest brown sugar, they are warm, and dry, and comfortable. The tiniest infant can turn them with a spade; they are never covered by the sea in summer time, and there are miles and miles of them, stretching to the right hand and to the left. What is the consequence? They are popular as no seaside playground is popular. They are seized upon as "pitches" by the itenerant vocalist and photographer, they are like a fair from morning until night. The boatmen summoning recruits for a sail out to sea in painted luggers; the bathing men and women continually drawing the machines up and down the soft sand: the fruit sellers and sweet sellers, the try-your-weight machines and electric batteries, the gypsies and fortune-tellers, the flower-girls and cake men, give Yarmouth sands a character all their own. Yarmouth, as at present constituted, is the veritable home of music-hall minstrelsy. Songs and choruses go on from morning until night. An enterprising firm of singers with a harmonium and indefatigable perseverance has rented from the Corporation a ring of ground in the centre of the beach, and here they give concerts, open-air al fresco concerts, almost every day, depending for remuneration on penny chairs and programmes. On one of the principal piers there is a twopenny concert under a wooden shed all the morning before lunch, and almost all the evening after dinner, where the fashion of Yarmouth repairs to gather the latest flowers from the music-hall bouquet. There is no pride about the visitors here. A roughly painted pier, an old sail to keep off the wind, and a wooden shanty to shield them from the sun is quite enough for them, and they seem delighted with the sentiment and humour of the modern ballad. There is another pier, where a more refined entertainment is given, and classical music is introduced, at sunset, but it is not nearly so popular a concert as the one where the sentimental young ladies, over their books and knitting, join in the chorus to "Old Familiar Faces," when the old ladies weep over that heart-rending appeal, "Don't put my father's picture up for sale," or when the irresistible comic singer creates a furore with some intoxicating refrain. But even here the full skill of the music-hall minstrel is not exhausted, for the crowds that have sung these songs all the morning on the sands or on the Britannia Pier will be found at night at the Aquarium vociferously applauding the "lion comique" before unlimited dancing winds up the pleasures of the day. This is the one, and possibly the only, watering-place that has no select or fashionable quarter. Margate boasts its Cliftonville, and Ramsgate has her Granville or Marina, places where it is possible to get away from the cheerful and laughter-loving crowd. But at Yarmouth you are bound to do as Yarmouth does. You must in the morning thread your way amongst the thousands of children who are doing on the sands what children have done from time immemorial. You will find them making castles and moats and tunnels; you will see them constructing a sand armchair for mother and father, and burying their nursemaids and sisters in this comfortable grit; you will watch them contentedly filling their shoes, and eyes, and hair with sand, and eating their sandy luncheons out of sandy newspapers. It is no exaggeration to say that children swarm on the Yarmouth sands as they swarm nowhere else in England. The beach is perfectly safe; they can all paddle and dig and roll without the slightest danger. If aweary of watching these childlike amusements, you must go out for a two-hours' sail, or be found on the sea in some shape or size of boat at some period of the day or other. This is *de rigueur*. On one occasion I was watching over the pier-head a party of excursionists tossed upon the waves and sadly sea-sick. Their condition was so heartrending that a friend called out in compassion to the leader of the party, "I say, old boy, aren't you coming in?" "No!" replied a melancholy and sea-sick voice, "Oh, no. We've got half an hour more!" This determination not to be done out of half an hour's abject misery struck me as heroic but none the less comical. From the fascinating sands of Yarmouth it is impossible to tear the great bulk of the visitors. There are excursions in the immediate neighbourhood to Cromer, to Lowestoft, to Southwold, and up the river to Norwich; but to the sand and the piers the holiday-makers remain faithful. Here all day they dig, and bathe, and boat, and idle, and sing; as night comes on they sing again, and dance at the Assembly Rooms or Aquarium, and one and all eat oysters before they go to bed. This oyster eating is an institution in Yarmouth. There are oyster stalls underneath the music platform on the pier, oyster stalls permanently attached to the most popular hotels on the sea front, and as nightfall comes on perambulating stalls make their appearance, a wide tray covering a costermonger's truck, and lighted by swinging lamps, affording rather a pretty effect along the sea front and the fringe of these delighful sands.

But the full value of Yarmouth as a playground for the people was practically shown to me. A well known firm of manufacturers at West Ham—one of the most crowded among

East-end districts—had arranged an excursion for the whole of their work people, as they have been in the habit of doing for several years past. These imprisoned toilers who have so little light and air at home have been taken continually to Rosherville and the Crystal Palace and such like places, but this year it was arranged to carry them all down to Yarmouth, nine-tenths of them never having seen the sea in their lives. The excursion was arranged on the most liberal scale. Not only those actually employed at work, but their wives, their mothers, their fathers, and their babies were included in the invitation. By accident I saw the arrival of these six hundred excursionists at the railway station, and followed them as they rushed joyously in a great army to the sea. In the train they were singing at the top of their voices; they sang in the streets as they were directed seaward; but the sight of those sands and the sea fairly astounded them. They simply rolled about the sands with sheer delight as children do on a meadow. They had no spades to dig with, or buckets to fill, but they scraped out holes for themselves with their hands, and then flung themselves down, revelling in the fresh air and blue sky. After a pause they were on the move again, singing and shouting at the top of their voices, and clambering into the boats to go out to sea, to feel what the waves were like, to get the breeze full on their faces. Luckily the sea was calm, and they returned none the worse to the dinner and tea that had been provided for them at the Aquarium, within a stone's throw of the sands. But so long and wide are the Yarmouth sands that this important addition made no appreciable difference. Though all these excited enthusiasts were flung upon the hospitable shore, not a child was disturbed in digging, and not a sand castle was knocked down.

Yarmouth, though unattractive at first in a purely picturesque sense, grows upon the visitor. He will not find here fashionable promenades or a very select society; people do not come here to dress or to show their high-heeled boots; they come to enjoy the air and to get health, to brown their skins, and to bathe the baby. The air blows clean and soft full from the German Ocean; there is health in every step taken from the Nelson Column to the North Battery. There are prettier bits of coast away by Gorleston and its quaint old pier to which fashion is more inclined, but for honest simplicity, unconventionality, and general comfort commend me to honest Yarmouth—the people's playground by the sea.

A ride on the sands.

The Year's End at an Old Farm.

WHEN the last day of the old year comes upon us, and we are sensible of another change in our lives, the sentiment of the occasion is due to the individual and not to society at large. In London, as in other cities, the year dies and another one succeeds it almost unheeded. We go on buying and selling; the shops are open and crowded with customers; the theatres are gay with the first flow of children to the Christmas pantomimes; the same noise, the same confusion, the same worry and unrest, continue as they did on any given day in any given year. There is little solemnity in the manner of bidding farewell to an old year, be it bad or good. Round and about us there are few signs either of regret or thankfulness; there is no ceremonial of pathos or hilarity. A stranger coming into London on New Year's Eve would not be able to distinguish it from any other important day of the week or year. All goes on as usual. The streets echo with the roar of ceaseless traffic, the passengers go hurrying or jostling one another on the pavement, dense fogs and mists still cling "like a face-cloth on the face" of a saddened city, and, so far as outward appearances go, if there be any effort to mark the last moments of the dying year, it is one of studied indifference and neglect. The individual, however, cannot divest himself of the idea that something ought to be done to remember what is passing and what is to come. Each one in his own way stands somewhere or other at the grave of the dying year. One takes down his desk and remembers absent friends; another goes silently off to the midnight service, to kneel in silence and whisper a prayer for those in trouble and those at rest. Some there are who join hands round a convivial bowl, and sing "Auld lang syne;" others go quietly downstairs and, opening the street door, as the bells ring out, clasp hands in silence, looking out into the dark streets, but very far beyond them in imagination. All that happens in the family circle may be conventional, but the greetings are sincere. When the door closes and the clock has struck, a weight seems to have been lifted off the heart. Absolution has been pronounced.

We face life free again. The least superstitious people, those who care very little who first crosses the threshold of their houses on New Year's morning, cannot help feeling that there is a change in their daily lives. They will have to date their letters a new way to-morrow morning. A new croupier has sat down at the gambling-table of life. Luck, somehow or other, may change.

But whatever individuals may do—whether they go to the church and say their prayers, or stay at home and entertain their friends, or empty the punch-bowl, or take hands on the door step, or write letters, or sing songs, whether they forgive or forget, it is impossible for anyone to remain unimpressed by the year's farewell as it may be seen out of London, far away from the town, in the heart of the country where no noise prevails, and where little merriment is heard.

There is a sadness in the very atmosphere, charged as it were with tears of moisture. Grey rain-clouds hang mournfully over a landscape wholly in the minor key. The hedges, bare and leafless now, show drops of water on every twig; the skeleton grasses in the undergrowth glisten with exquisite diamond dust of dew. A few months ago the farmland was warm and ruddy, the earth turned up red and brown to the advancing plough, the ferns framing the coppice were bright and golden, the green of the root crops gave to the landscape a certain brightness and life. All is changed now. The earth is black, the oversoil is sad and grey, the roads are melancholy and muddy. A green Christmas, as it is called, sounds prettily enough when it is spoken ; it is not, however, so picturesque to the eye. It means that the first-sown wheats are being choked with rank grasses and foul weeds, that the carters cannot get along the lanes to carry manure to the fields, that the soil is so heavy and so dead with wet that the farmer is almost in despair. He would like just now to welcome a light bright frost, hard enough to pulverise the soil for the sowing and to make the lanes and the roads accessible for his heavy waggons, constantly employed between the farmyard and the distant fields on the estate. Come, then, into the farm garden, and see if you can find any flowers there, come to the old white gate where we sunned ourselves in the summer-time. The inside of the old farmhouse looks bright enough this New Year's Eve, but Art has supplied what Nature has denied us. A great mass of colour in the centre of the parlour first attracts the eye; yellow and brown and red and deep green. Examine closely, and you will find that careful and skilful fingers have been stitching holly berries and immortelles and golden everlastings upon the shining holly leaves and upon the bare stalks with surprising effect. Never did the farmhouse look so cheerful. A great bunch of evergreen greets the visitor in the doorway, the pictures and window frames are decorated with twigs of holly, and across the walls of the best sitting-room runs a device of welcome made of yellow everlastings on a groundwork of pink calico. Outside, the prospect is not so cheerful. The garden that used to smile in the sunshine with phlox and verbena and geranium looks as if it had been trampled on and crushed under foot. The white farmhouse gate has turned stone grey with the moisture that hangs on it. There is a brave collection of dead stalks and leafless shrubs. Surely there must be one flower left here in this old farm garden, where we saw the corn ripen under the mill such a short time ago, as it seems; there must be something to remind us of the past. Yes, there are three flowers left. Down the small avenue of the apple trees a tuft of chrysanthemum, terra-cotta red, has lived on right up to the last day of the old year; one blackened rosebud is still as true to the famous bush by the farmyard gate that looked so beautiful last summer, and best of all, as it seems to-day, up in a warm corner, under an old moss-covered wall, may be found just two clots of early primrose, the pretty advance guard of the flower army of the coming spring. Elsewhere there is nothing but death, decay, and desolation. Up the lanes towards the sea you may wander and find little life but the ever-green of the holly in the leafless hedge, and just one hidden bunch of yellow gorse to show that Nature has a smile left upon her face.

At this old farmhouse by the sea it is indeed the end of the year. Time's destiny is written on the very face of the landscape. There is no need for church bells to ring, or clocks to strike, or for any sign to show us that the death-hour has come. Let us mount together to the cliff's edge, close by the deserted churchyard and the ruined tower, high up where the poppies grew so luxuriantly in the ripening corn, let us stand side by side at the old corner, where there used to be spread for us such a garden of wild flowers. Is this the sea, so silent and so still, stretched out like a grey and waveless lake before us? Imagination cannot reconcile a winter sea with such a scene. There is not a footprint on the blackened sand; there is not a ripple upon the silence of the waters. A grey sky, a dark and flowerless land, a sea of inexpressible sadness. It is the close of the year, and it looks, as we stand lost in imagination, like the end of the world. In summer time the children used to laugh as they played under the broken wall of the ruined churchyard; later on, the harvest men sang and shouted at their work as they flung the wheat into the waggons, fearful of the advancing storm. But now there is no sound either on sea or land. The soil is so soft you cannot hear the cutting of the plough, the children have gone down from the cliffs to the village, and only two sailors are standing at the cliffs' edge looking out to sea, but saying nothing. There have been sunsets elsewhere of surpassing beauty—green and orange, and crimson and gold. But here on the brown cliffs there cannot be a sunset, for there has been no sun. The grey morning changes to the greyer afternoon; the curtain slowly falls, and then comes the night. Walking along the cliffs' edge this New Year's Eve, over the grass down, past the white lighthouse tower, it seems like a recollection in a dream. It is te same and yet not the same. Not a human being has apparently been here since the summer time. The gay wild flowers, yellow and scarlet, are dead, the ferns are blackened and seemingly burnt into the mossy grass so often trodden by the happy visitors of the little seaside holiday home who loved to come up here from the village. The turf is light and springy, but the gaiety is gone. Here are the names of the lovers cut into the turf in a bye-path, just as they were left; here are the footprints of sand shoes in the soft ground at the edge of the cliff. Look down upon the beach and see what desolation. Not a boat, not a yacht, not a target, or a bathing machine. What a merry village it used to be, every hole and corner full, children scrambling up the paths, girls with streaming hair fresh from their morning bath. Where are they now? The lodging houses are boarded up, the hotels are empty. The stranger who comes down from the cliff and enters the village is taken for a ghost of the departed summer. So homeward, still together, past the lighthouse, throwing its rays now on the deserted country, now on the lonely sea. The night creeps on, and the melancholy is more and more intense Apparently the villagers do not care much about the passing of the old year. It is early yet, scarcely theatre time in London, but already there are lights in the upper windows and signs that the villagers intend to sleep the end of their year away. At last the farm is reached in the darkness. There is not even the faint glimmer of a moon to guide us homewards. Hour succeeds hour. The farmhouse clock strikes eleven, but not a soul is stirring. No carols, no songs, no sound of revelry anywhere in this forgotten corner of the world. Listen for the sound of church bells and you will not hear an echo. The village is asleep; the ringers are in bed. The old miller is dozing over his open Bible, his wife sits by his side and gazes into the fire; the little daughter trims the lamp anew and waits. Let us go out into the darkness, lean over the old farm gate, and hear the silence.

It is silence everywhere; silence across the lonely fields, silence on the lonelier sea; no light in any window, no sparkle or star in the darkened heavens; nothing of life and hope but the flash and the gleam of the lighthouse on the sea down miles away. Listen again, and try if you can hear a bell or a clock strike. Nothing but silence. Far off, a dog barks in a distant farm. It is the time now. Listen again; do you hear nothing? Nothing; no moan, no whisper. There is no breath or pulse in the old year. He has gone. Thank God we were together at the passing hour! Is there nothing more to be said out here by the old farm gate, nothing more to be done? Nothing but hope and the future, nothing but the complete unity that is the very sweetness of life. On the lighted table by the side of the new year's fire, as we return from the darkness, a volume of Ruskin's "Modern Painters" lies open, strangely enough, at the following passage, descriptive of unity:—"And the unity of earthly creatures is their power and their peace. Not like the dead and cold peace of undisturbed stones and solitary mountains, but the living peace of trust and the living power of support—of hands that hold each other and are still!" Thus upon the old year's tombstone we both write "Finis!" and together we journey onwards still into the land of shadows!